Lars Brownworth is an author, speaker, broadcaster, and teacher based in Maryland, USA. He has written for the Wall Street Journal and been profiled in the New York Times, who likened him to some of history's great popularizers. His books include *The Sea Wolves: A History of the Vikings; In Distant Lands: A Short History of the Crusades;* and *Lost to the West: The Forgotten Byzantine Empire that Rescued Western Civilization.*

The Normans

From Raiders to Kings

LARS BROWNWORTH

First published in the United Kingdom in 2014
by Crux Publishing Ltd.

ISBN: 978-1-909979-08-6

Copyright © Lars Brownworth, 2014

Also available as an ebook:
eISBN: 978-1-909979-03-1

Requests for permission to reproduce material from this work
should be sent
to hello@cruxpublishing.co.uk

For Nils, whose curiosity provided the spark

.

CONTENTS

People and Places   ix
The Papal States   xv
On Romans, Holy Romans, and Byzantines   xvi
The Hautevilles   xviii
Maps   xix

Introduction   1

Prologue: The Viking Age   7

1. The Northman's Duchy   11

2. Building a Dukedom   18

3. Inventing the Normans   23

4. The Magnificent Devil   30

5. Duke William   38

6. The Anglo-Saxon Kingdom   50

7. The Conquest of England   60

8. Bras de Fer   71

9. Guiscard   83

10. The Imperial Crown   93

11. Bohemond I   104

12. Dextera Domini   121

13. Rogerios Rex   137

14. William the Bad   161

15. William the Worse   173

16. The Monkey King   189

17. Stupor Mundi and the Norman Sunset   200

Epilogue: The Norman Legacy   213

List of Emperors   216
List of Popes   219
Bibliography   221
Endnotes   223

PEOPLE

Adelaide (c. 1075 – 1118) Third wife of Roger I and mother of Roger II. Regent for her son from 1101 – 1112

Alexius Comnenus (c. 1056 – 1118) Byzantine emperor at the time of the First Crusade. Defeated attempts by Robert Guiscard and Bohemond I to invade the empire

Bernard of Clairvaux (1090 – 1153) Cistercian Abbot and dominant figure of the early 12th century

Bohemond I (c. 1058 – 1111) Eldest son of Robert Guiscard; founded the Principality of Antioch

Charles the Fat (839 – 888) Frankish king who attempted to stop Viking raids by allowing them to settle in Normandy

Christodulus (d. 1131) First admiral of Norman Sicily under Roger II

Constance (1154 – 1198) Sister of Roger II; inherited Sicily when William the Good died

Count Roger (c. 1031 – 1101) Youngest of the Hauteville brothers; conquered Sicily and consolidated Norman rule of the island. Also known as the 'Great Count'

Drogo de Hauteville (c. 1010 – 1051) Younger brother of William Iron-Arm who succeeded him as Duke of Apulia and Calabria

Edward the Confessor (c. 1003 – 1066) Anglo-Saxon king of England who died without a clear successor

Emma (c. 985 – 1012) Sister of Duke Richard II; wife of Ethelred the Unready and mother of Edward the Confessor

Ethelred the Unready (c. 968 – 1016) Anglo-Saxon king who tried to stop Viking raids by bribing them. Father of Edward the Confessor

Frederick I Barbarossa (1122 – 1190) Holy Roman Emperor; invaded Italy in an attempt to conqueror Sicily

Frederick II Barbarossa (1194 – 1250) Holy Roman Emperor and King of Sicily and Jerusalem; Son of Henry VI and grandson of Roger II. Nicknamed 'the wonder of the world'

George Maniaces (d. 1043) Byzantine general who employed Norman mercenaries in an attempt to conquer Sicily

George of Antioch (d. 1151/2) Succeeded Christodulus as admiral; helped establish a Norman presence in North Africa

Godwin (Earl of Wessex, c. 1001 – 1053) Powerful advisor to Edward the Confessor and father of Tostig and Harold

Gregory VII (c. 1015 – 1085) Reforming pope who offered Robert Guiscard legitimacy in exchange for protection against Henry IV

Harald Hardrada (c. 1015 – 1066) Viking King of Norway; invaded England in 1066 and died at the Battle of Stamford Bridge

Harold Godwinson (c. 1022 – 1066) Last Anglo-Saxon king of England. Killed by William the Conqueror at the Battle of Hastings

Henry IV (1050 – 1106) Holy Roman Emperor who tried to invade Rome while Robert Guiscard was occupied by Byzantium

Henry VI (1165 – 1197) Holy Roman Emperor and husband of Constance; conquered the Norman Kingdom of Sicily

Maio of Bari (d. 1160) Favorite of William the Bad; most powerful figure in Sicily until his assassination

Manuel Comnenus (1118 – 1180) Last strong Byzantine emperor of the 12th century; campaigned against Roger II

Margaritus (1149 – 1197) Admiral of Sicily under William the Good; nicknamed 'the new Neptune'

Pope Leo IX (1002 – 1054) Led a great anti-Norman coalition to expel the Normans from southern Italy; captured by Robert Guiscard at the Battle of Civitate

Pope Urban II (c. 1042 – 1099) Launched the First Crusade to recover Jerusalem for Christendom

Raymond of Toulouse (c. 1041 – 1105) Main rival to Bohemond I for leadership of the First Crusade

Richard the Fearless (933 – 996) Son of William Longsword; first Duke of Normandy

Richard the Lionheart (1157 – 1199) Norman king of England who visited Sicily en route to the Third Crusade

Richard II (c. 962 – 1026) Second Duke of Normandy; also known as 'Richard the Good'

Robert Guiscard (c. 1015 – 1085) Half-brother of Drogo; conquered much of southern Italy and was elected Duke of **Apulia and Calabria.** Known as 'The Crafty'

Robert the Devil (c. 1009 – 1035) Third Duke of Normandy, father of William the Conqueror

Roger Borsa (c. 1060 – 1111) Legitimate but ineffectual son of Robert Guiscard; succeeded his father as Duke of Apulia and Calabria

Roger II (1095 – 1154) First Norman king of Sicily; remembered as its greatest ruler

Rollo (c. 860 – 931) Viking raider who founded Normandy

Tancred de Hauteville (c. 980 – 1041) Poor Norman knight and founder of the Hauteville family; father of at least twelve sons including William Iron-Arm, Drogo, Robert Guiscard, and Count Roger

Tancred of Galilee (1075 – 1112) Nephew of Bohemond I; regent of Antioch in Bohemond's absence

Tancred of Lecce (d. 1194) Last Norman ruler of Sicily; seized the kingdom when William the Good died. Nicknamed 'the Monkey king'

Tostig (c. 1026 – 1066) Younger brother of Harold; killed at the Battle of Stamford Bridge while attempting to return from exile

William Iron-Arm (c. 1005 – 1046) Eldest of the Hauteville brothers; elected Duke of Apulia and Calabria

William Longsword (c. 900 – 942) Son of Rollo; second ruler of Normandy

William the Bad (1131 – 1166) Son of Roger II and second king of Sicily

William the Conqueror (c. 1026 – 1087) Illegitimate son of Robert the Devil, conquered England in 1066

William the Good (1155 – 1189) Third king and last legitimate Hauteville ruler of Sicily

PLACES

Aachen: Capital of the Holy Roman Empire

Apulia: Region of southern Italy including the 'heel' of the peninsula. Became the center of Norman power under Robert Guiscard

Byzantine Empire: (330 – 1453) The eastern half of the old Roman Empire

Calabria: Region of southern Italy forming the 'toe' of the peninsula

Constantinople: Capital of the Byzantine Empire

Holy Roman Empire: (962 – 1806) Central European State that claimed to be the rebirth of the old Western Roman Empire. Despite its name it was based largely in modern day Germany

Norman Kingdom of Sicily: (1130 – 1194) Founded by Roger II; included Sicily, the south of Italy, and parts of North Africa

Palermo: Capital of the Norman Kingdom of Sicily

Papal States: Collection of lands around Rome ruled directly by the pope. Often in conflict with its immediate neighbors, the Norman Kingdom of Sicily and the Holy Roman Empire

Principality of Antioch: (1098 – 1268) Crusader State

based around the major city of Antioch; founded by
Bohemond I during the First Crusade

VARIOUS

Battle of Civitate: (1053) Norman defeat of the armies of
Pope Leo IX; resulted in papal recognition of Hauteville rule
in southern Italy

First Crusade: (1096-1099) Launched by Pope Urban II to
reclaim the Holy Lands from Islam

Fourth Crusade: (1204) Venetian-led crusade which sacked
Constantinople

Treaty of Saint-Clair-sur-Epte: Agreement between Rollo
and Charles the Simple that created Normandy

Varangian Guard: Elite forces of the Byzantine army.
Usually composed of Norse or Anglo-Saxon warriors

THE PAPAL STATES

When the Western Roman Empire collapsed in the fifth century, it left a political vacuum on the Italian peninsula. The pope, virtually the only figure of significant standing, gradually filled the void, assuming political control over Rome. In 756 this *de facto* control was made official by the Frankish ruler, Pepin, who had recently defeated a Lombard invasion that threatened Rome. In exchange for the title of king, Pepin 'donated' his newly-conquered lands surrounding the two cities of Rome and Ravenna to the pope. The resulting Papal States (also called the Republic of Saint Peter) were ruled directly by the popes until the nineteenth century when they were dissolved during the *Risorgimento* (unification of Italy).

The exact borders and power of the Papal States fluctuated considerably during the middle ages. At their greatest extent they covered the modern central Italian regions of Lazio, Umbria, Marche, and part of Emilia-Romagna. This territory was guarded by the papal armies, which were commanded in the field by mercenaries, or on occasion, by the pope himself. This period of papal history is best represented by the Renaissance pontiff, Julius II, who built an army around a core of Swiss mercenaries and gained the epithet *the Warrior Pope* for his frequent military excursions.

After the unification of Italy in 1871, the pope's temporal power was restricted to the walls of the Vatican compound, but even that was in doubt. In 1929, an accommodation was reached with the Italian government, which recognized an independent state of 'Vatican City'. It is still protected by Julius' Swiss Guard, a remnant of the time when popes fought temporal – as well as spiritual – wars.

ON ROMANS, HOLY ROMANS,
AND BYZANTINES

Clarity about the past is often sought by oversimplifying it. History is broken down into digestible chunks with neat borders and labels which, however useful, can sometimes be misleading. Dates which were hardly noticed at the time become watershed years, and epochs and ages are given names which would have been unrecognizable to those living during them.

When national or imperial pride gets involved, the resulting propaganda usually muddies the water even further. The Middle Ages had two rival empires both claiming to be the true Roman Empire. For most of their history neither of them actually controlled Rome, yet both had claims on its legacy.

The confusion stems from the third century AD when the Roman Emperor Diocletian decided to split the old Roman Empire in half. The western half, with its capital in Italy, collapsed in the fifth century (the traditional date is 476), but the eastern portion survived until 1453 when a Turkish invasion and the guns of the modern world finally brought it down.

Since the eastern half was centered on Constantinople, the old Greek city of Byzantium (modern day Istanbul), modern historians refer to it as 'The Byzantine Empire' or simply 'Byzantium'. Its location in the thoroughly hellenized east meant that Greek became the preferred language, so Byzantium is sometimes referred to as the Greek empire. Nonetheless, it is important to note that while it existed, both friends and enemies alike viewed it as Roman, and drew no artificial distinctions between the empire of Rome and that of Byzantium.

The medieval competitor to the 'Byzantine' Empire arrived on Christmas Day in the year 800. During a Mass in Rome, Pope Leo III (for political reasons of his own) placed a crown on the Frankish king Charlemagne's head and named him Imperator Romanorum, announcing that the defunct Western Empire had been reborn. This version of the empire, however, which spanned both French and Germanic lands, was based in present day Germany and never completely controlled Italy. Because of this, and in an attempt to simplify a complex series of events, most historians refer to Charlemagne's coronation anachronistically as the start of the Holy Roman Empire or the German Empire. Politically, Charlemagne's state fell apart almost immediately, and when his direct line petered out in less than a century, the title of Roman Emperor soon followed it. In 962 the German Otto I (a distant relative of Charlemagne) revived the title, and in 1157 his successor Frederick Barbarossa officially added the term sacrum (holy) to his title.

This German-speaking, Holy Roman Empire may have been – as Voltaire put it – neither 'holy', nor 'Roman', nor (since the emperor was elected) an 'empire' – but it was resilient. It survived until the nineteenth century when, in a fit of Enlightenment pique, Napoleon swept it away.

For clarity's sake I refer to the Greek-speaking eastern empire as 'Byzantine', and the German-speaking western one as 'German' throughout the book.

THE HAUTEVILLES

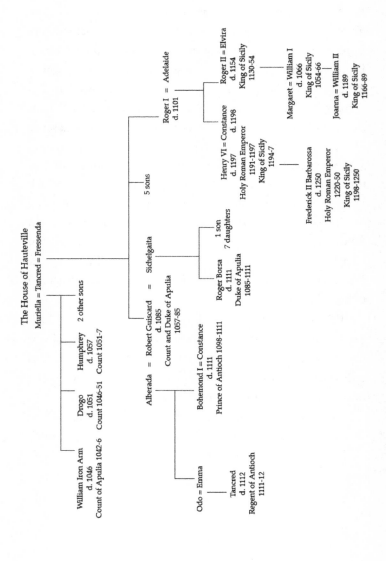

The House of Hauteville

Muriella = Tancred = Fressenda

William Iron Arm
d. 1046
Count of Apulia 1042-6

Drogo
d. 1051
Count 1046-51

Humphrey
d. 1057
Count 1051-7

2 other sons

Alberada = **Robert Guiscard** = Sichelgaita
d. 1085
Count and Duke of Apulia
1057-85

Roger I = Adelaide
d. 1101

Odo = Emma

Bohemond I = Constance
d. 1111
Prince of Antioch 1098-1111

Roger Borsa
d. 1111
Duke of Apulia
1085-111

1 son
7 daughters

5 sons

Roger II = Elvira
d. 1154
King of Sicily
1130-54

Tancred
d. 1112
Regent of Antioch
1111-12

Henry VI = Constance
d. 1197   d. 1198
Holy Roman Emperor
1191-1197
King of Sicily
1194-7

Margaret = **William I**
d. 1066
King of Sicily
1054-66

Frederick II Barbarossa
d. 1250
Holy Roman Emperor
1220-50
King of Sicily
1198-1250

Joanna = **William II**
d. 1189
King of Sicily
1166-89

NORMANDY & ENGLAND C.1066

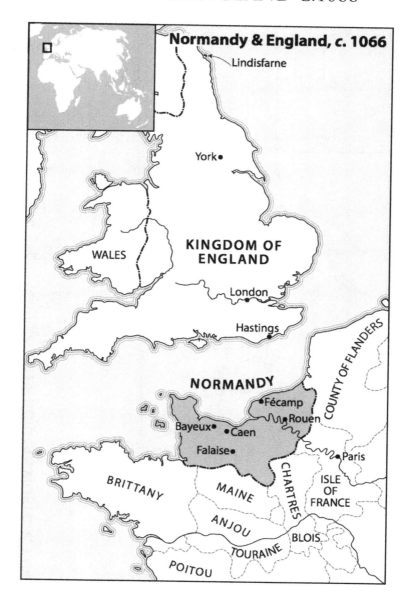

Normandy & England, *c.* 1066

Lindisfarne

York

KINGDOM OF ENGLAND

WALES

London

Hastings

COUNTY OF FLANDERS

NORMANDY

Fécamp

Rouen

Bayeux

Caen

Falaise

Paris

BRITTANY

MAINE

CHARTRES

ISLE OF FRANCE

ANJOU

BLOIS

TOURAINE

POITOU

THE NORMAN WORLD C.1100

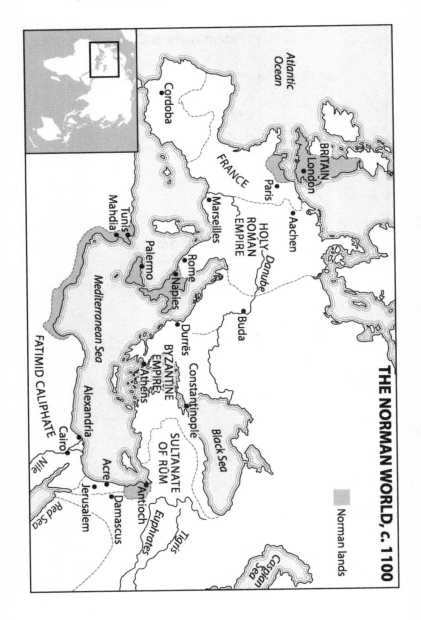

CRUSADER KINGDOMS c.1135

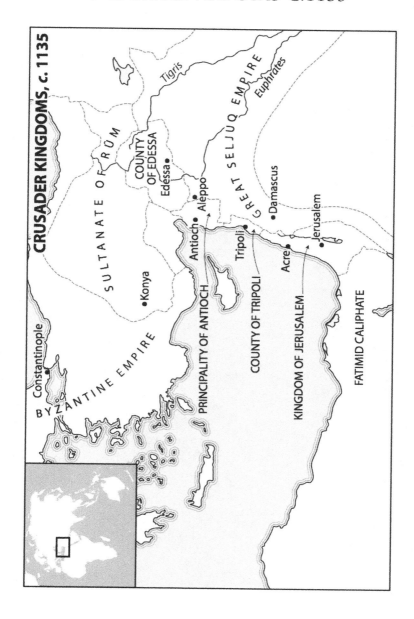

CRUSADER KINGDOMS, c. 1135

SULTANATE OF RÚM

•Konya

Constantinople

BYZANTINE EMPIRE

PRINCIPALITY OF ANTIOCH

COUNTY OF TRIPOLI

KINGDOM OF JERUSALEM

FATIMID CALIPHATE

COUNTY OF EDESSA

Edessa•

Antioch •

Tripoli •

Acre •

Jerusalem

• Aleppo

• Damascus

GREAT SELJUQ EMPIRE

Tigris

Euphrates

PAPAL STATES C.1200

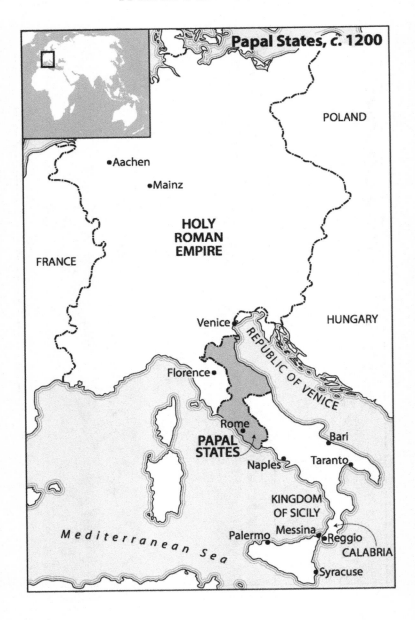

Papal States, *c.* 1200

POLAND

•Aachen

•Mainz

HOLY
ROMAN
EMPIRE

FRANCE

Venice•

REPUBLIC OF VENICE

HUNGARY

Florence •

Rome•

PAPAL
STATES

Bari•

Naples•

Taranto•

KINGDOM
OF SICILY

Messina•

Palermo•

Reggio•

CALABRIA

Syracuse•

Mediterranean Sea

INTRODUCTION

The idea for this book began with a question: How did Western Europe, which was militarily, technologically, and socially far behind its immediate neighbors in the Middle East, manage not only to catch up with them, but to rise to global dominance?

At the start of the second millennium, a gambler certainly wouldn't have placed their bet on the West. It was much more likely that the sophisticated and sprawling Islamic Caliphate would continue to dominate, or perhaps the cultured, resurgent Byzantine[1] Empire. Europe was a battered shell, crumbling under the hammer blows of invasion and disease. And yet, it was a group of Viking descendants – the very ones who were ripping Western Europe apart at the time – that would provide the catalyst for its future greatness.

Few events in European history are as remarkable as the sudden rise of those Normans in the latter half of the eleventh century. In the space of a single generation they carved out kingdoms from the North Sea to the North African coast, and transformed Europe. They lived in a world where the old order was passing away and the clever among them had seemingly unlimited possibilities. For the bold no ambition was too lofty, and no dream was impossible. They were among the West's first great entrepreneurs; a powerful example that in the new world of the tenth century low birth was no bar to success.

But who exactly were the Normans? Despite their prominence, there is an air of ambiguity to them. They settled in France and can most famously be seen on the Bayeux Tapestry, but were not strictly French. Their most famous king ruled over England so they can just as easily be called English, but they can also be seen as Norse, or even Italian. Even their legacy is conflicted. They appear in the story of Robin Hood as oppressive villains, and at the same time are regarded as the founders of the English state who established modern law and eliminated slavery.

One of the reasons for the confusion is that the whole Norman story is not widely known. The Norman identity is dominated by William the Conqueror, the illegitimate son of an absent father, who famously landed at Pevensey Beach in 1066 and conquered the Anglo-Saxon kingdom of England.

There is another Norman conquest, however, which is in some ways even more remarkable. Six years before Duke William launched his invasion, the sons of an impoverished Norman knight headed south, creating a kingdom that extended from southern Italy to the Tunisian coast. Full of the restless ambition of their Viking ancestors, they presided over a century of commercial expansion that turned Palermo (in present day Sicily) into the cultural and economic capital of the western Mediterranean. Most importantly, they fostered the rising fortunes of the papacy at a critical period in the history of Christendom, playing a pivotal role in the formation of a European identity.

It was an astonishing achievement for men with such humble beginnings. Tancred de Hauteville, an obscure Norman knight living in northern France, had little he could offer his twelve sons and most left to seek their fortunes in the south. They arrived as humble mercenaries, but quickly proved to be among the most inspired of medieval leaders. From William 'Iron-Arm' who killed the Emir of Syracuse in single combat, to Robert Guiscard who captured a pope and nearly overthrew the Byzantine Empire, the sons of Tancred combined ambition with tenacity. For three quarters of a century they carried out a systematic campaign to enlarge their territories, culminating with Count Roger who accepted the unconditional Saracen[2] surrender of Sicily and adopted the dress and customs of a Byzantine emperor. By the time the youngest Hauteville brother died, his relatives sat enthroned in Palermo, Tripoli, Malta, and Antioch, and the family possessed the strongest and wealthiest kingdom in Europe.

The Hauteville family, however, is important for more than just colorful individuals. They are also part of a larger Norman story, embodying the energy of a continent poised for rapid growth. At the start of the eleventh century, Europe was largely agrarian, politically divided, defensive, and economically undeveloped. Three non-European powers – the Byzantine Empire, the Spanish Caliphate, and the Fatimid Caliphate of Cairo – dominated the Mediterranean. England was part of the Scandinavian cultural orbit, Rome was mired in the corruption and politicking of the early papacy, and Christendom was under attack from the formidable powers of Islam.

Within a generation of the arrival of the Normans, much of Europe was transformed from a collection of feuding states to a culturally united and politically strong region. In place of a patchwork of French fiefdoms, they created an Anglo-Norman empire, stretching from Scotland to the Pyrenees. In Italy they found Lombard, Byzantine, and Saracen princes controlling a confused array of provinces, and replaced them with a single Norman kingdom. The Byzantine Empire was driven out of Italy, the Saracens were expelled from Sicily, and a revived papacy began the Western offensive against Islam that would spawn both the Reconquista and the Crusades.

Norman power also coincided with several more fundamental shifts. From the eleventh century to the twelfth, the population of Europe nearly doubled. With a larger workforce came a greater specialization of labor, the founding of guilds, and technological innovations like the windmill and stern-mounted rudder. The growth of cities and towns encouraged the formation of communes and the first medieval experiments with democracy. Trading organizations like the Hanseatic League brought the West into contact with the Byzantine and Islamic worlds and partially reintroduced Europe to Greek learning and advances in medicine and science. The new Gothic form of architecture began to spread from France to the rest of the continent, and with it came a reform movement fostered in Norman monasteries that resulted in a revival of learning broad enough to be called the Renaissance of the twelfth century. Vernacular literature emerged, Latin poetry and Roman law were revived and the first European universities were founded. Lastly, the stability that the Normans gave to the Italian peninsula allowed the reforming pope, Gregory VII, to spread his idea of a universal Christian society far beyond Italy – and with it the concept of a united Europe.

In each of these movements, a Hauteville played a catalyst role, sparking events that would begin the European rise to dominance on the world stage. Yet for all their accomplishments, the southern Normans remain largely unknown, eclipsed by their famous northern compatriots. Knowledge of the Normans for far too many seems to begin and end with the Battle of Hastings, while the Hauteville's central role in the growth of Europe is largely unexplored.

This is somewhat surprising, because the brothers are the most prominent example of the Norman genius of adaptability that transformed Europe. They had the instinctive ability to recognize which local traditions were superior to their own and to combine the various cultural and legal elements into a cohesive whole. Perhaps because they were a cobbled together people themselves, they displayed this pragmatic streak in every place they inhabited.

The first Normans were Scandinavian Vikings hopelessly outnumbered amid a French population, and they quickly learned how to govern a people without alienating them. In Sicily, the Hautevilles perfected this skill. They kept the existing structure of the Muslim and Byzantine administration intact combined it with French efficiency and gave Sicily a prosperity it hadn't seen since the days of imperial Rome. The former mercenaries transitioned into southern kings, exchanging war for trade and mercantile activity. At the time of the First Crusade, when Christendom was internally divided and at war with Islam, Roger de Hauteville protected the Sicilian Kingdom with an army composed of Saracen infantry, Greek generals and Norman cavalry. His example provided a template for the Hauteville governance of Sicily, and the great cathedrals of Cefalù and Monreale, with their fusion of Norman, Islamic and Byzantine architecture, are still a testament to the success of his efforts.

This story needs to be restored to its proper place in the history of European development. Unlike the Norman Conquest of England, the Hautevilles did not have the backing and resources of a dukedom. Their progress was slow – the conquest of Sicily alone took over thirty years of sporadic fighting – and the obstacles they had to overcome were daunting. Yet in the end their determination paid off, and their success proved enduring. They were a blend of ambition, greed and daring that was often repellent but never dull. In the most unlikely of places – the center of the Mediterranean

– they created a bridge between East and West Christian and Muslim, ruling with an effectiveness that was unparalleled in the Middle Ages and has rarely been equaled since. They played a crucial role in explaining how the West emerged from the chaos of the early Middle Ages to a place of global prominence, and took the first steps in creating the modern world. This is their story.

Prologue

THE VIKING AGE

Nostra conservando corpora et cutodita, de gente fera
Normannica nos libera, quae nostra vastat, Deus, regna

(Preserve us and ours, O God, from the savage race of
Northmen which lays waste our realms)

– Antiphony of St Vaast or St Medard (c. 870)

In the year 793 the monks of Lindisfarne priory were interrupted from their evening meditations by an astonishing sight. Fiery dragons appeared in the night sky, wheeling menacingly above the island monastery before vanishing into the darkness. Sheets of lightning followed, spreading out in vast arcs above the priory roof, outlining the building with an unearthly flame. A few weeks later the dragons returned, but this time they were carved into the prows of ships. When they beached, wild men carrying strange rune-covered swords came swarming out, overtaking the monks before they could flee to safety. Neither the old nor the infirm were spared as the cloister was ravaged. Gold and silver plate was seized, precious vestments were torn from their hangings, and even the ossuaries were smashed open in search of valuables. When there was nothing left to plunder, the invaders loaded everything into their ships and departed as quickly as they had come, leaving behind the corpses scattered

– as a cleric later wrote – like so much dung in the streets.

It was only a taste of the storm to come. For the better part of the next two centuries the Viking onslaught broke on northern Europe, ripping apart kingdoms and leaving coastal cities almost deserted. The brutal assault was made worse by the thoroughly alien nature of these Norse warriors from Scandinavia. Unlike the majority of people in Western Europe they weren't Christianized; they recognized no church sanctuary and showed no mercy. Worshiping their terrible berserker[3] god Odin, the one-eyed, raven deity that inspired divine madness, these hulking warriors didn't seem to feel pain and would attack with teeth and nails when their weapons were gone. Clothed in the skins of wolves or bears, they appeared like some bestial scourge from the frozen north.

These cunning warriors were no mere brutes though, and were capable of remarkable sophistication. Thanks to a clever Viking innovation in shipbuilding that eliminated the need for a keel, they could sail up even the shallowest rivers, and it was this mobility that made them truly lethal. Even inland cities, long thought to be safe from seafaring raids, were now in range.

There seemed to be no limit to their wanderlust. Sailing to the west, Norse adventurers colonized Iceland, Greenland, and eventually, as is now generally recognized, the New World. In Ireland they founded the city of Dublin, in Muslim Spain[4] they seized the city of Seville, and in Africa they raided the Moroccan coast. Cruising up the coast of Italy they sacked the largest city they could find, and returned to Scandinavia boasting that they had conquered Rome. The fact that it was actually Luna, center of the Italian marble trade, was beside the point. No city was safe.

The Anglo-Saxon kingdom of England was among the first to be buffeted by the storm. Viking raiders overran York, captured London, and butchered at least two English kings[5] as a sacrifice to Odin. Other Vikings sailed east and found their way to the Black Sea, where they were daring enough to try an attack on mighty Constantinople. Called the 'Rus' by the Byzantines, these Vikings carved out settlements among the Slavic populations of northeastern Europe and gave their name to the land of Russia.

A major target of Viking activity was what today is northern France. The Norsemen were interested in loot, and there was no more tempting target than the Frankish Empire.

By the year 800, it looked as if the great western dream of restarting the Roman Empire had become a reality. The Frankish king, Charlemagne, had hammered together the lands of France, Germany, Switzerland, and northern Italy into a single state, and the pope had crowned him emperor of this new Roman Empire[6]. Trade flourished, learning was revived, and wealth poured into Frankish treasuries. Charlemagne built a magnificent palace at his capital of Aachen, dazzled his subjects with a court that seemed to drip with gold, and even toyed with the idea of marrying the Byzantine empress in a bid to unite the lands of the old Roman Empire. At his death in 814 it looked as if the Mediterranean-spanning Pax Romana would dawn again under Frankish leadership.

Unfortunately for the Franks, none of Charlemagne's successors ever quite measured up to him, a fact made painfully obvious by the nicknames their depressed subjects gave them. Charlemagne's first son got the best of the lot as Louis the Pious, but it went downhill from there. After Louis came Charles the Bald, Louis the Stammerer, Charles the Fat, Louis the Blind, and so on.

Guided by these feeble rulers after the death of Charlemagne and hopelessly divided, the Frankish lands were both

wealthy and weak, a lethal combination which quickly attracted the attention of the predatory Vikings. By the end of the
century the attacks had become so frequent that many coastal
towns had to be abandoned, and even Paris was briefly occupied. The helpless Frankish kings, unable to match Viking
speed, resorted to a disastrous policy of bribing the invaders
to leave, but this only bankrupted the treasury and convinced
the Vikings that the Franks were indeed weak. In 880 the ul-
timate humiliation occurred when Charlemagne's old capital
of Aachen fell to the invaders, and its citizens were forced to
watch as Viking horses were stabled in the magnificent palace
chapel. The Frankish king responded to the crisis (as he did to
most others) by sending a massive payment of gold and silver,
and the now fabulously wealthy Vikings lumbered off, strug-
gling to carry all their loot.

This victory marked a subtle change in Viking tactics. By
now their thoughts had turned from plunder to settlement,
and the northern seacoast looked particularly inviting. There
was little to fear from the Frankish military; Vikings could
besiege even major cities with virtual impunity. The difficulty
lay in choosing an appropriate spot at which to settle. The
Norse were men of the sea – they were often called 'sea wolves'
by their victims – so any permanent location had to have easy
access to water. Paris and Aachen may have been rich targets,
but they were too far from the coast to make suitable bases.
Ironically, it was a Viking defeat, not a victory, which provided
the perfect location.

Chapter One

THE NORTHMAN'S DUCHY

The entry for the year 885 in the French Annals of St Vaast begins with the chilling phrase: "The rage of the Northmen was let loose upon the land". It was an all-too-accurate assessment. As soon as the winter snows had melted, a frenetic series of Viking raids hit the French coast and continued with a ferocity not seen for half a century. This particular year was especially demoralizing because the Frankish population had believed that they had gained the upper hand against the raiders. Four years earlier, the Franks had met the Norse in a rare pitched battle and slaughtered some eight thousand of them. For several years the threat of attack had receded, but then in 885 the Norse launched a full-scale invasion.

Viking attacks were usually carried out with limited numbers. They were experts in hit and run tactics, and small bands ensured maximum flexibility. That November, however, to the horror of the island city, more than thirty thousand[1] Viking warriors descended on Paris.

From the start, their organization was fluid. According to legend, a Parisian emissary sent to negotiate terms was unable to find anyone in charge. When he asked to see a chieftain he was told by the amused Norse that 'we are all chieftains'. There was a technical leader – traditionally he is known as Sigfred –

but not one the Franks would have recognized as 'king'. It was less of an army than a collection of war bands loosely united by a common desire for plunder.

The Vikings launched an attack hoping to catch the French off guard, but several days of intense fighting failed to break through the Parisian defenses. The resulting siege, which lasted for a year, was ultimately unsuccessful, but it gave Europe its first glimpse of the man whose descendants would dominate both ends of the continent, and whose distant relative still sits on the English throne. Known to posterity as Rollo (the Latin version of the Norse Hrolf), he was a minor leader, probably of Norwegian[2] extraction. According to legend he was of such enormous size that the poor Viking horses couldn't accommodate him[3], and this earned him the nickname Rollo the Walker (Hrolf Granger), since he had to go everywhere on foot.

Like all the Vikings, Rollo had been drawn to the siege by the very real prospect of making a fortune. Forty years before, the legendary Norse warrior Ragnar Lodbrok had sacked Paris with fewer men, returning home with nearly six thousand pounds of silver and gold courtesy of the terrified French king. All of those present had undoubtedly been brought up on stories about Ragnar's exploits, and there may even have been a veteran or two among the gathered warriors. This was their chance to duplicate his exploits.

If Rollo distinguished himself at Paris, it was in his determination. When it became apparent that an early victory wasn't possible, many of the Norse began to drift away towards easier targets. By March of the next year, morale among the Vikings was so low that the nominal leader, Sigfred, reduced his demand to sixty pounds of silver – a far cry from Ragnar's six thousand – to lift the siege. However, a rumor that the Frankish emperor, Charles the Fat, was on his way with a relief army stiffened the will of the Parisians and they refused. Sigfred held out another month, and then gave up, leaving Rollo and the other lesser leaders on their own.

The Frankish army finally arrived in October, eleven months after the siege began, and scattered what was left of the Vikings. Rollo's men were surrounded to the north of Paris at Montmartre, but Charles the Fat decided to negotiate instead of attack. The province of Burgundy was currently in revolt, and Charles was hardly a successful military commander. In exchange for roughly six hundred pounds of silver, Rollo was sent off to plunder the emperor's rebellious vassal.

It was an agreement that suited both of them, but for Rollo, the dream of Paris was too strong to resist. In the summer of 911 he returned and made a wild stab for it, hoping smaller numbers would prevail where the great army had failed. Not surprisingly, Paris proved too hard to take, so Rollo decided to try his luck with the more reasonable target of Chartres.

The Frankish army had been alerted to the danger and they marched out to meet the Vikings in open battle. A ferocious struggle ensued, but just when the Vikings were on the point of winning, the gates flew open and the Bishop of Chartres came roaring out, cross in one hand, relic in the other, and the entire population streaming out behind him. The sudden arrival turned the tide, and by nightfall Rollo was trapped on a hill to the north of the city. The exhausted Franks decided to finish the job the next morning and withdrew, but the crafty Viking was far from beaten. In the middle of the night he sent a few handpicked men into the middle of the Frankish camp and had them blast their war horns as if an attack were underway. The Franks woke up in a panic, some scrambling for their swords, the rest scattering in every direction. In the confusion the Vikings slipped away.

With the dawn, the Frankish courage returned, and they hurried to trap the Vikings before they could board their ships, but again Rollo was prepared. Slaughtering every cow and horse he could find, the Viking leader built a wall of their corpses. The stench of blood unnerved the horses of the arriving French, and they refused to advance. The two sides had reached an effective stalemate, and it was at this point that the French king[4], Charles the Simple, made Rollo an astonishing offer. In exchange for a commitment to convert to Christianity, and a promise to stop raiding Frankish territory, Charles offered to give Rollo the city of Rouen and its surrounding lands.

The proposal outraged Frankish opinion, but both sides had good reason to support it. The policy of trying to buy off the Vikings had virtually bankrupted the Frankish Empire. More than a hundred and twenty pounds of silver had disappeared into Viking pockets, an amount which was roughly one-third of the French coins in circulation. There was simply no more gold or silver to mint coins, and the population was growing resistant to handing over their valuables to royal tax collectors. Even worse for Charles, the Viking raids had seriously undermined his authority. It was impossible for the sluggish royal armies to respond to the Viking hit and run tactics, and increasingly his subjects put their trust in local lords who could offer immediate protection rather than some distant, unresponsive central government. The authority of the throne had collapsed, and now it was the feudal dukes who held real power. If Charles allowed another siege of Paris he would lose his throne as well. Here, however, was a solution that promised to make all the headaches go away. Who better to stop Viking attacks than the Vikings themselves? By gaining land they would be forced to stop other Vikings from plundering it. The nuisance of coastal defense would be Rollo's problem, and Charles could focus on other things.

For his part, Rollo was also eager to accept the deal. Like most Vikings he had probably gone to sea around age fifteen and now, perhaps in his fifties, he was ready to settle down. Local resistance was becoming stronger, and there was little more to be gained in spoils. After decades of continuous raiding the coasts were virtually abandoned, and wandering further inland risked being cut off from the ships. This was an opportunity to reward his men with the valuable commodity of land and to become respectable in the process. Rollo jumped at the chance.

The Treaty of Saint-Clair-sur-Epte, as it came to be known, created the Terra Normanorum – the land of the Northmen. This treaty of the Northman's Duchy, or Normandy, was formally agreed to at a meeting between the two protagonists. The Viking warlord agreed to be baptized together with his entire army, and to perform the ceremonial act of homage to King Charles. Unfortunately, this last part was carried out with a certain lack of grace.

The traditional manner of recognizing a feudal lord was to kiss the royal foot, but Rollo wasn't about to do any such thing. When Charles stuck out his foot, Rollo ordered one of his warriors to do the deed for him. The huge Norseman grabbed the king's foot and yanked it up to his mouth, sending the hapless monarch sprawling onto his back. It was, had they only known, a fitting example of the future relationship of the Norman dukes to their French overlords.

Charles hoped that his grant of land was a temporary measure that could be reclaimed later. Such things had been done before and they never lasted beyond a generation. In Rollo, however, he had unwittingly found a brilliant adversary.

Rollo instantly recognized what he had; a premier stretch of northern France with some of the finest farmland in the country. His genius – and that of his descendants – was a remarkable ability to adapt, and in the next decade he managed to pull off the extraordinary feat of transforming a footloose band of raiders into successful knights and landowners.

Rollo understood, in a way that most of those around him did not, that to survive in his new home he had to win the loyalty of his French subjects. That meant abandoning most of his Viking traditions and blending in with the local population. He took the French name Robert, married a local woman, and encouraged his men to do the same. Within a generation the Scandinavian language had been replaced by French, and Norse names had virtually died out.

However, the Normans never quite forgot their Viking ancestry. St Olaf, the legendary Scandinavian king who became Norway's patron saint, was baptized at Rouen, and as late as the eleventh century the Normans were still playing host to Viking war bands. But they were no longer the raiders of their past, and that change was most clearly visible in their army. Viking forces fought on foot, but the Normans rode into their battles mounted. Charges from their heavy cavalry would prove irresistible, and carrying the Normans on a remarkable tide of conquest that stretched from the north of Britain to the eastern shores of the Mediterranean.

One final change took longer to sink in, but was no less profound. Christianity, with its glittering ceremonies and official pageantry, appealed to Rollo probably more out of a sense of opportunity than conviction. His contemporaries could have been forgiven for thinking that Odin had given way to Christ suspiciously easily[5]. The last glimpse we get of Rollo is of a man hedging his bets for the afterlife. Before donating a hundred pounds of gold to the Church, he sacrificed a hundred prisoners to Odin.

Christianity may have sat lightly on that first generation of Normans, but it took deep root among Rollo's descendants. There was something appealing to their Viking sensibilities about the Old Testament – even if the New Testament, with its turning the other cheek wasn't quite as attractive – and they took their faith seriously. When the call came to aid their oppressed brothers in the East, they would immediately respond; Norman soldiers provided much of the firepower of the First Crusade.

When Rollo finally died around 930, he left his son an impressive legacy. He had gone a long way towards turning his Viking followers into Normans, and turning an occupied territory into a legitimate state. For all that, however, troubling clouds loomed on the horizon. Normandy's borders were ill-defined, and it was surrounded by predatory neighbors. Its powerful nobles had bowed to the will of Rollo while he was alive, but they saw little reason why they should extend the same loyalty to his son. Most worrisome of all was the French crown, which eyed Rouen warily and was always looking for an excuse to reclaim its lost territory.

Rollo had laid the foundation, but whether Normandy would prosper, or even survive at all, was up to his descendants.

Chapter Two

BUILDING A DUKEDOM

Rollo's death left the young duchy at a crossroads. Succession from father to son wasn't an established fact, and while Rollo's eldest child William Longsword – by now a thirty-four-year-old veteran – was the obvious candidate, Viking leadership had to be won.

Although Rollo had been the unquestioned leader, his last years hadn't been triumphant. Expansion to the East had largely been stopped by the powerful neighboring Count of Flanders, and William Longsword proved to be a handy scapegoat. Several rebellions against his authority had to be brutally suppressed before he could assert control. Much of the resistance came from his adoption of the surrounding culture. Rollo may have encouraged the embrace of local traditions, but William abandoned his heritage with unseemly haste. He married a direct descendant of Charlemagne, swore fealty to the French king, and had even started calling himself 'Count of Rouen'.

This last bit was typical Norman bluster. The title that the treaty of Saint-Clair-sur-Epte accorded was a simple Latin 'princeps', in this case nothing more than the generic 'leader'. By adopting a Frankish title, William not only confirmed his subjects' worst fears about his Gallicizing tendencies, but also alarmed Arnulf, the formidable Flemish count.

The struggle to halt the Norman advance had been a hard one, and Arnulf had no desire to see it begin again under an ambitious new leader. When William made the mistake of intervening in Flemish politics, Arnulf decided to permanently destabilize the troublesome province. Pretending that he wanted to make peace, he lured William to an island to discuss their differences, then had him assassinated.

Not content with merely killing its leader, Arnulf twisted the knife further by then inviting the French king, Louis IV, to invade. William's son, Richard I, was only nine years old, and clearly incapable of any organized resistance. The armies of Louis and Arnulf swept into Rouen, took Richard hostage and sent him off as a trophy to the king's court.

That would have been the end for Normandy if it were not for the mutual disgust King Louis and Arnulf felt for each other. Before long, Arnulf had withdrawn in a huff, and without Flemish support Louis' position was hopeless. When a Norman force counter-attacked Rouen, he not only lost the battle but managed to get himself captured in the process. The delighted Normans exchanged him for their captive count, sending the humiliated monarch back to his capital, chastened, if not wiser. Richard I returned to Rouen in triumph, and at the tender age of thirteen took control of his inheritance. He ruled for the next forty-nine years.

The problems facing the new count were enough to demoralize a grown man, but he threw himself into his work with a heedless abandon that earned him the nickname 'the Fearless'. He quickly proved far more adept on the Frankish stage than his father had ever been. When the French king decided to threaten Normandy again, Richard invited some Danish Vikings to pillage the upper Seine Valley. After a few weeks of such treatment the king got the message and offered peace. Richard, however, wanted a more permanent solution. The Carolingian kings descended from Charlemagne would always be hostile to upstart Normandy, so he helped an ambitious noble named Hugh Capet to seize the throne, helping to establish the Capetian line of kings that would last for over three hundred years. All in all, it was a stunning reversal of fortune for one who had started his political career as a prisoner of a Carolingian king.

Richard next turned his attention to internal affairs. One of the duties of a Christian prince was to look after his subjects' spiritual well-being, and the church in Normandy was in an appalling state. The turmoil of the previous century had left most of its monastic houses abandoned, and driven priests from their parishes. Over the next few decades Richard re-founded monastic communities at Mont St-Michel, Fécamp and Evreux, and imported reforming monks from across Europe to fill them. As a signal of how important the Church was he even appointed his younger son to the See of Rouen – a tradition that virtually every reigning member of his family would continue. Since education was largely in the hands of the church, literacy slowly began to recover. It is mostly from his foundation at Fécamp that we get the earliest records of the Norman dynasty.

As Norman prestige grew with the influx of clergy, Richard gradually became dissatisfied with the title of 'Count'. At first he tried out the old Roman 'Consul' then switched to the more formal 'Marquis'. Soon, however, he had his eyes on an even more prestigious appellation. Hugh Capet had been a Duke – a title reserved for the greatest of the Franks – and since he had vacated it on assuming the mantle of king, Richard appropriated it for himself. Neighboring chroniclers (rolling their eyes no doubt) referred to him as the 'Duke of the Pirates', but nonetheless, the title stuck.

By the fall of 996 Richard the Fearless had spent half a century in power and was in failing health. At sixty-three he had lived longer than most of his contemporaries and few expected him to survive much longer. While in Bayeux he fell ill and moved to his favorite castle in Fécamp. There he solemnly chose a successor and walked barefoot to the nearby abbey where he received communion and asked to be buried under its portico. The next night a sudden seizure struck him and he was dead by the time his attendants reached him.

He had been a formidable duke, and Normandy owed much of its firm foundations to him. While Normandy had been largely Christianized and feudalized under his leadership, perhaps his greatest accomplishment had been to convince his Scandinavian subjects that the principle of legitimacy, of son succeeding father, was far preferable to the instability of rule by the strongest.

His reign is also the great dividing line in early Norman history. Documentation on the reigns of Rollo and William Longsword is shadowy at best, long on legend and short on facts. Thanks to Richard's patronage of the Church, however, the monks returned to their Chronicles, and contemporary accounts multiplied. With Richard the mists of legend part and Normandy emerges into the historical record.

The Normans certainly appreciated their long-lasting duke; they virtually canonized him. He was remembered glowingly as a sustainer of the poor, a guardian of orphans, a defender of widows and a redeemer of captives. Later legends even had him wandering Rouen at night, confronting demons outside dark churches. The greatest tribute to him, however, was composed a century after his death. In the Song of Roland, the great French epic about Charlemagne, he appears as 'Richard the Old', complete with long white beard and clear, alert eyes.

Normandy of course didn't exist at the time of Charlemagne, but thanks to Richard, by the time the poem was written, France without a Normandy seemed inconceivable to the French.

Chapter Three

INVENTING THE NORMANS

If the Normans gained a duke with Richard the Fearless, they gained an identity with his son. Oddly enough, this was in large part due to the kingdom of England. While the Norman role in the creation of modern England is well known, most are unaware that the reverse is also true. England played a crucial role in the creation and defining of Normandy.

The British Isles had not only born the brunt of the first Viking raids in the eighth century but had proved so tempting to the Norse that a great Viking army had invaded with the intention of completely conquering it. The Anglo-Saxons were hampered by the fact that they were split into several kingdoms at the time (seven is the traditional number) and within a few years the Vikings had managed to conquer all but the southern kingdom of Wessex. It seemed only a matter of time before that fell as well, but fortunately for the Anglo-Saxons, the king of Wessex was a brilliant strategist named Alfred and he managed to fight the Vikings to a standstill. During his reign he turned the balance of power in his favor and slowly but surely pushed back the Norse invaders. He was so successful that he earned the epithet 'the Great', the only English monarch to accomplish that thus far. Alfred's greatest accomplishment, however, was that he convinced the Vikings that England was no longer a land of such easy pickings. As a result, the next wave of invaders, which included the adventurer Rollo, decided to try their luck in France.

Alfred's grandson Æthelstan continued his father's efforts, even extending English control into Scotland where he received the submission of the Scottish king and declared himself 'King of all Britain'. Under a strong monarchy, commerce replaced raiding, and by the time Richard I was reigning in Normandy, England was fabulously wealthy. It did not, however, have a surplus of leaders, as the English were quick to find out.

A fresh wave of Viking activity hammered northern Europe and the British Isles, and the English king Ethelred fell back on the tried – and disastrous – method of buying the Norse off. This won him the unflattering nickname 'Ethelred the Unready'[1]. Raiders that had come in search of plunder discovered an endless supply of easy money. All they had to do was burn a few villages and wait for the king's representative to show up with gold to buy them off

Ethelred's treasury couldn't handle the strain of constant Viking payments, so he levied a special tax called the 'danegeld' (literally 'Viking money') to pay for it. This would possibly have been acceptable to the common man (who was paying it) had it been effective, but the danegeld only made things worse. Not only was it tremendously expensive, but since it tended to draw invaders instead of discourage them, it was also completely demoralizing.

Across the Channel in Normandy, Duke Richard I was facing the lesser but related problem of what to do about the Vikings. Despite their shared cultural heritage, the last thing the Norman duke wanted was a group of uncontrollable Vikings upsetting trade and rampaging through his territory. A succession of Norman leaders had done their best to convince the rest of Christendom that they were civilized Christians; Richard could hardly welcome pagan raiders into his territory and maintain that pretense. What's more, there was also nothing to guarantee that the Vikings wouldn't turn on him. They wanted plunder and Normandy had plenty of it.

Richard was still wondering what to do when the Vikings forced his hand by requesting access to his ports to sell the goods they had plundered from England. The aging Richard was caught in a dilemma: actively resist and draw Viking ire or assist them and confirm the dark rumors already swirling that the Normans were nothing more than pirates themselves.

Perhaps it was because he still felt a distant kinship to the Norse, or perhaps he was trying to avoid becoming a target himself, but for whatever reason, Richard I opened the ports and braced himself for the inevitable controversy.

It erupted almost immediately. The English in particular were horrified that a fellow Christian prince was providing hospitality for the very raiders that were despoiling their nation, and sent an appeal to the pope to bring the Normans back into line. The pope was reluctant to do this as he was, at the time, engaged in a struggle to reform the Church and the Normans were great patrons of reform in their territory, but the scandal was so intense that a papal representative was dispatched to Richard, and the duke reluctantly signed an agreement to stop harboring Ethelred's enemies. He could hardly break off relations completely, however; he instructed his merchants to continue trading and five years later he died, leaving the issue for his son to deal with.

Although the thirty-three-year-old Richard II was technically illegitimate, it was a smooth transition of power; a testament to how deeply the principle of succession had taken root. Important marriages were always political matches, and the Norman dukes took the same approach to their mistresses, living openly with them and considering their offspring legitimate. The general population seems to have accepted this as a relic of the old pagan days and been content enough to let such things slide. It was fortunate that there were no real challenges to his authority, for Richard II was soon faced with his first real test.

Drawn by decades of easy English loot, a huge Danish army descended on Wessex in 996 and began a three-year systematic plundering of the kingdom. By the time Ethelred had gathered enough money to persuade them to leave, the Vikings had decided that they needed a base from which to continue further attacks. They asked Richard II for permission to use Norman ports to resupply.

Richard was caught in the same quandary as his father, and he came to the same conclusions. In England, Ethelred the Unready was starting to panic. He had emptied the treasury to force the Vikings away, only to see them get what he assumed was a friendly reception across the Channel and continue their attacks. He had to find some way to close Norman ports. An appeal to the pope proved ineffective, so the king tried his hand at diplomacy. Richard II had an unmarried sister named Emma, and Ethelred offered to marry her if the Normans agreed to shut the door to the Norse.

This was too good an opportunity for Richard to miss and was certainly worth the risk of offending the Vikings for, so young Emma was packed off to London. Confident that he had solved the Viking menace at last, king Ethelred carried out a surprise massacre of the Danes living in the southwest of England and then mustered a huge fleet to hold off any Danish retribution. When some months passed with no Viking attempt at revenge, Ethelred put his navy to use settling some old scores. Richard II may have been a useful recent ally, but the Normans had stood by for years while the Norse tormented England. The time had come for a little payback,

so a detachment was sent to raid the coast of Normandy. It
was easily routed, but by then Ethelred had larger problems.
The Danish massacre had given its king, Svein Forkbeard, the
perfect excuse to invade. Since Richard II had been needlessly
antagonized, Svein was welcomed to Rouen with open arms.
After a formal alliance between the two was concluded and
an oath of perpetual peace sworn, Svein continued to England
where he found surprisingly little resistance. The English were
tired of their weak king and since Svein was already a Christian
he wasn't met with the usual suspicion accorded to Vikings. By
the end of the year the Dane was sitting on the English throne
and Ethelred, Emma, and their two young sons were living in
awkward exile in Normandy.

Richard II seems to have realized rather quickly that he had
gone too far in making a treaty with the Vikings. Norman dukes
had always tried hard to pretend that they were proper French
nobility, but the surrounding people were deeply suspicious of
their Norse ancestry. Now, it seemed as if the Norman inner
Viking was revealed for all to see. Proper Christian, French
princes didn't go around making treaties with Viking kings
or trading with Viking pirates – and they certainly didn't use
Viking mercenaries to threaten other Christians.

Richard had recently been guilty of just this. He got
involved in a border skirmish with Brittany, and had brought
in Norse warriors[2] to help him, which scandalized popular
opinion among the surrounding French. Nearly as bad (in the
French view) as the shameful behavior of duke Richard II was
the conduct of his sister Emma. Barely two years into her exile
both her husband Ethelred and his rival Svein Forkbeard died,
and she wasted no time abandoning her young sons to marry
the new Viking king of England. The boys, one of which was
the future king Edward the Confessor, were left to fend for

themselves, effectively disowned and orphaned.

Normandy was clearly being drawn into the Scandinavian orbit, proving what the Gallic population had long suspected about its half-civilized new neighbors. In order to refurbish the tarnished Norman image, Richard II commissioned a pro-French history of the duchy. What better way to combat negative public relations than with a little spin of his own?

Norman history was given a thorough white-washing. Rollo acquired a high birth in Norway; his fierce son William Long-sword was transformed into a gentle ruler – a monk at heart and a lover of peace who died a martyr's death. Richard I was made a paragon of virtue, fighting equally to reform the Church and maintain his independence from the powerful north.

The tendency of the dukes to have public mistresses was rather embarrassing, but they were given the title 'Danish wives' and explained away as holdovers from the old Norse, pagan days when rulers didn't know any better. Even Richard II's mother got a makeover. In reality she was the daughter of a powerful vassal of Richard I who had become the duke's mistress to cement ties with her father. Now, however, she became a humble forester's daughter who met the duke by chance on a hunting trip and captured his heart with her beauty and virtue.

These were ancestors that an ambitious duke needed, worthy of even the proudest French nobility, and they gave Richard II the credibility he desired. From his court at Rouen he handed out titles, appointing viscounts, seneschals, and constables in a quantity that not even the king of France could match. All of a sudden Norman forces seemed to be everywhere, intervening in neighboring squabbles, pressing ducal claims, and expanding the territory of Normandy. The message Richard was sending was clear: these were the actions of one of the great lords of France, and even if uncrowned, he was nearly the equal of the king.

By the time he died of natural causes at the ripe old age of sixty-four, Richard II had successfully managed to turn the perception of Normandy as a rogue Viking state into one of the most powerful provinces of France. He was a friend of the French king, the brother-in-law of the English king, and had at least five grown sons to carry on his line. His subjects remembered him fondly as Richard the Good, and might possibly have done so without the pandering of court historians. More than any other duke, he had been responsible for creating an identity for his people, and had laid the foundation for even greater heights yet to come.

Chapter Four

THE MAGNIFICENT DEVIL

The death of a medieval ruler was always an invitation to chaos, but Richard had made excellent preparations for his succession. There was no shortage of available heirs to choose from since the late duke had two brothers and five sons. The eldest son, Richard III, was the obvious choice, and was groomed from the start. When his father died, he was thirty years old, popular, battle-tested, and, most importantly, he already had a son to ensure the next generation of dukes. The various other uncles and siblings were bought off with extensive states around Normandy, and everybody was perfectly content to settle down and enjoy their new arrangements.

The only one unhappy with the new situation was Richard III's younger brother, Robert, who at seventeen was cocky, energetic, and absolutely convinced that he should be the one in charge. His share of the inheritance was an estate in central Normandy focused around a castle in Falaise, and from the security of these walls he loudly announced his fitness to rule to anyone that would listen. When neither of his uncles showed the slightest interest in backing him, he decided to revolt anyway, and started ravaging his way through the countryside.

Richard III was in no mood to take any abuse from his little brother and he swept into Falaise at the head of his army, forcing Robert to go scampering back to his castle. To the latter's horror, Richard then produced siege engines and methodically reduced its defenses. Robert was forced to make a humiliating public act of submission, and returned chastened to Falaise to rebuild his favorite castle.

Richard's triumph over his brother set the stage for an even greater diplomatic coup. The king of France had an infant daughter, and as a mark of Richard's preeminent status, she was betrothed to him, but just as the young duke was making preparations for his wedding, he fell ill and died. Poison was immediately suspected as the cause of his death, and, although no one was foolish enough to say it to his face, everyone suspected Robert. His aspirations were well known, and his behavior hardly broadcast innocence. Almost before his brother's body was cold, Robert had moved into the palace and shipped Richard's young son off to a monastery to keep him safely out of the way.

The incident (not altogether fairly) earned the new duke the nickname Robert the Devil. Medieval society was notoriously susceptible to diseases, any number of which could strike without warning, but to the medieval mind, sudden death was among the most terrifying of fates. A sudden death meant that there was no time for preparations, confession, or ritual, leaving the victim unprepared for the terrible Day of Judgment. So awful was this demise that a particularly vicious medieval curse was 'May you die without warning!' When one of the powerful met their end unexpectedly, the suspicion was that such a thing couldn't have occurred naturally. The explanation usually depended on an individual's popularity. Corrupt or wicked rulers were struck low by the divine hand, while the promising were invariably poisoned.

Robert may have stood to benefit the most from his brother's death, perhaps he even wanted him dead, but that's hardly an airtight case for poisoning. His actions in seizing the duchy could be attributed to ambition and pragmatism as much as guilt, and by moving quickly and firmly he had undoubtedly prevented further bloodshed. Furthermore, although his reputation was certainly damaged, and rumors of his use of poison dogged him for the rest of his life, no one – not even Richard III's cloistered son Nicholas – seemed to have a problem with Robert taking control. As a later Norman historian blandly summed it up 'Robert was given the duchy by hereditary right'.

It was one thing to gain power, however, and quite another to rule. Robert had taken every opportunity he could to encourage the aristocracy to stir up trouble against his brother, and now he was plagued by rebellious nobles. Unauthorized castles started popping up and church lands were confiscated, but he was too busy punishing those who had failed to support him from the start to do anything about it. His uncle, who also happened to be the archbishop of Rouen, had failed to rush to his side in his first revolt and now the time had come for a little payback. Marching into his protesting uncle's territory, the duke unceremoniously expelled him from Normandy, and confiscated his property. Encouraged by this easy victory, Robert next turned on his cousin, the Bishop of Bayeux, sending another hapless relative into exile.

This seizure of Church property didn't go unnoticed by the pope in Rome, where Robert's banished uncle, the archbishop, was arguing for all of Normandy to be put under interdict, a case that was strengthened by the duke's behavior. Protesting clergy were continually ignored and sent packing, and word of their suffering eventually trickled down to Rome. Finally the pope acted and Robert was excommunicated.

The duke was cut off from the sacrament, forbidden from

receiving remission of his sins. If he died under this sentence he would be prohibited from being buried in consecrated land, and his bones would be doomed to molder outside the blessings of the church. The excommunicate was an outcast from society; all feudal bonds of loyalty were dissolved. Nobles no longer needed to obey the command of an outcast duke, and any that gave him shelter ran the risk of bringing the church's condemnation upon themselves.

News of the dreadful sentence was brought to the duke in Falaise where he was staying in his favorite castle, but he was too distracted to pay much attention. He had just met an extraordinary woman named Herlève.

The daughter of a tanner, Herlève was spotted by Robert while he was walking on the roof of his castle. Legend has it that she was assisting her father by walking barefoot on the garments that were being dyed, holding her dress up to keep it clean. When she noticed the duke's attention she coyly lifted her skirts a bit higher, dazzling Robert with a view of her legs. Smitten, the duke ordered one of his men to quietly fetch her, instructing him to bring her through the back door directly to his chambers. Herlève, however, announced that she would either come proudly through the front gate or not at all. The obsessed duke caved in and Herlève rode proudly up to the castle on a white horse, dressed in her finest clothes. If she was going to be the duke's mistress, then she would be his only one, and make sure that everyone knew it. Nine months later she presented Robert with a son, and the pleased father named him William after the second duke of Normandy.

The difference in their social status made a marriage impossible, and Robert soon found himself under enormous pressure to marry her off to someone else and cease his association with her. A century earlier, a mistress wouldn't have been a problem, but the slow reform of the Church that his father and grandfather had encouraged had begun to reshape the morals of Normandy. Even more serious than this, however, was Robert's excommunication. Every day that passed endangered his mortal soul and even the hotheaded duke couldn't shrug off such pressure forever. Swallowing his pride, he recalled his uncle, the archbishop, and restored his property and land.

The move was the great turning point of his reign. Like Shakespeare's young Prince Hal, his reckless days were over, and he was determined to acquit himself as a proper duke. Herlève was provided with a husband, Church property that had been seized was returned, and an attempt was made to force various lawless magnates to do the same. The great religious houses in Normandy, especially Fécamp, were endowed at his personal expense, and placed under his protection.

The nobility resisted any attempts at centralization, but Robert kept them occupied by a vigorous foreign policy. When the Count of Flanders was exiled by his own son, Robert took advantage of the chaos to invade his neighbor, ostensibly to restore the old count, but in reality to extend his influence. The following year, Brittany threatened Mont St-Michel and Robert repeated the same tactics, forcing Brittany's count to publicly acknowledge his vassal status. In 1033 a palace coup sent the young French king, Henry I, into exile and handed Robert a golden opportunity to extend Normandy's reach. Henry fled to Fécamp, home of his most robust supporter, and requested the duke's help. An army was quickly mobilized and Robert swept towards Paris, crushing the rebel forces and restoring Henry to his throne.

The same year that saw Robert play kingmaker on the continent also brought opportunities across the English

Channel. The duke had close ties with the Anglo-Saxon royal family; his aunt Emma had married the English king, and her two sons, Alfred and Edward, were just slightly older than Robert. During Duke Richard II's reign, a Viking named Cnut had seized the kingdom, sending the three royals into exile in Normandy. They weren't together for long. Emma, ever the survivor, had returned to England to marry Cnut, abandoning her two sons to survive as best they could.

Duke Robert's cautious father had been somewhat indifferent to his English nephew's fate, but Robert was closer in age and moved by his cousin's plight. With characteristic flair he began to refer to the older sibling Edward as 'King of the English', and made the awkward demand that Cnut provide money for their upkeep. When Cnut laughed it off – he was hardly going to provide accommodations for a rival to his own throne – Robert followed up his threat by launching an invasion fleet.

This first attempt at a Norman conquest was more ad hoc than carefully executed. The fleet set sail in 1033 but ran into a storm and was quickly blown off course, landing further along the French coast in the middle of Brittany. Not one to waste the opportunity, Robert disembarked and led a quick raid through his neighbor's territory.

By the winter of 1034, Robert was twenty-five-years old and the most powerful magnate in France. He had corralled his vassals, dominated his neighbors, threatened one king and placed another on his throne – quite an accomplishment for a reckless younger son. He was at the height of his powers and appeared poised to become one of Normandy's strongest dukes. Then, at his Christmas court, he shocked everyone by naming his eight-year-old illegitimate son, William, as his heir, and announcing that he was leaving for Jerusalem.

There were the inevitable scandalized rumors, whispers that it was his guilty conscience that was spurring him to go, and that this was dramatic confirmation that he had poisoned his brother after all. In any event, whether it was guilt, adventure, or fatigue that drove Robert, he was determined to go. In a way, the destination was more astonishing than the idea of a pilgrimage itself. The more popular sites were Rome or Santiago de Compostela in Spain, and the road to Jerusalem was not only more expensive but far more dangerous, passing as it did through hostile Muslim lands. In 1027, however, a Byzantine emperor had reached an agreement with the Fatimid[3] ruler of Jerusalem guaranteeing the pilgrim routes and access to Christian shrines. As a result, traffic to the Holy Land had boomed, crowding the roads with the faithful who wanted to arrive just in time for the thousandth anniversary of the Crucifixion.

Robert had probably been thinking about the pilgrimage for some time. Leaving the duchy in the hands of a child was hardly the most responsible thing to do, but he had decided to go nevertheless, and made what arrangements he could. He had been slowly easing his son, William, into the role of heir, granting gifts and signing documents in his name. Now, at the Christmas court in Fécamp, he required his magnates to swear an oath of loyalty, something which they all did without exception or objection. Satisfied that he had fulfilled his obligations, Robert emptied his treasury and left Normandy forever.

He crossed the Alps and first headed for Rome, distributing so much gold to churches along the way that he was soon being called Robert the Magnificent. Had he gone just a bit further south he would have come across the first Normans who were trickling into the heel of Italy[4], but he most likely headed for the coast instead and took a ship for the East. He arrived in Constantinople some time early in 1035 making the most of his time by taking a tour of the city and even meeting the emperor who – in a bit of vanity on the part of Norman chroniclers – was supposedly impressed with his wealth. After mingling with the imperial court, the duke continued to Jerusalem, which he reached in time to celebrate Holy Week.

The city had plenty of ways for a pilgrim to spend money, and Robert took in all the sights, praying in the Church of the Holy Sepulchre and retracing the route Jesus walked on his way to the Crucifixion. His return trip was by all accounts equally pleasant. When he reached the Bosphorus in early summer, he paused at the charming little city of Nicaea. There he unexpectedly fell ill, and on July 2, 1035 he died. In a nod to his refurbished reputation a rumor started that he had been poisoned, and one Norman chronicler piously argued that God took him because he was 'too good for this world'.

His body was buried in Nicaea, where it was left until 1085 when a Norman delegation arrived to take it back home. They had only made it as far as Apulia, however, when word reached them that their current duke had also died, so they reinterred the body in Italy where it remains to this day.

Robert's brief reign had been a mixed success, and his wildly irresponsible departure for the east had virtually ensured civil war back home. Even worse, his failure to bring the powerful nobility to heel with anything more than a naïve oath had left his eight-year-old son William terribly alone, vulnerable to the far more experienced men around him. After nearly a decade of strong leadership, Normandy tipped back into chaos.

Chapter Five

DUKE WILLIAM

William the Illegitimate shouldn't have survived his childhood. Abandoned by his father at the tender age of eight, he was a helpless pawn in the dangerous game of Norman power politics. Pushed in front of a huge assembly of the great magnates of Normandy, probably bewildered and not quite understanding what was happening to him, he would have known only that his father was leaving. The men around him, barely concealing their hunger for his throne, would have provided little comfort, and most of the attention in any case must have been on Duke Robert as the various nobles tried to position themselves for his absence.

We have no record of the parting words between father and son – they were never to see each other again – but one hopes there was at least some attempt to soften the blow, probably mixed with some advice and an exhortation to be a man. Practical administration of the duchy would of course have been put in the hands of others, but William must have been terrified when the moment came, of both his father's absence and the weight of expectations. The sight of his father moving slowly away must have been among the loneliest feelings of William's life.

The danger of Robert's death to the stability of the duchy was mitigated somewhat by the time it took for news of it to filter back to Normandy. The duke left after the Christmas celebrations in 1034 and although he expired early the next spring, word didn't reach Normandy until August of 1035. By that time the Norman nobles had had nearly a year to get used to the idea of William as duke. Had Robert died at home, William could have been easily brushed aside – after all Robert himself had done exactly that to his own nephew when he seized power.

Despite his youth and inexperience, however, things weren't quite as bleak for William as they at first seemed. There were two important things working in his favor. The first was that all the various uncles, great uncles, and cousins who might have made a bid for the throne had all publicly accepted William as duke and sworn to support his claim. This meant that they couldn't openly break their allegiance without outraging popular opinion – and it undoubtedly saved his life. The second advantage was in his guardians. Robert had left a talented group of men to protect and shepherd his son through the minority of his reign. Chief among these was the archbishop, Robert, William's great uncle, the elder statesman of the family and the head of the Church of Normandy.

For two years Normandy was as stable as could be expected with power in the hands of a committee. The enormous prestige of the archbishop smoothed the transition, but there were limits to what the cleric could do and it soon became clear that William's father had frittered away much of the internal strength of Normandy. Past Norman dukes had understood that peace rested on a tamed aristocracy and had consequently strictly regulated where and when their vassals could build castles. During Robert's reign, however, that had almost completely broken down. Most of William's relatives were counts; all had lands loyal to them as well as multiple castles, and saw no reason why they shouldn't build more. With Robert's death having whetted the appetites of the ambitious, the nobility began expanding their power at William's expense. Unauthorized castles started springing up throughout Normandy, further weakening central authority, and there was little the child in Rouen or his advisors could do to prevent it.

Things worsened for William during the second year of his reign when his great uncle the archbishop, died. Without a man of such prestige to control them, William's remaining guardians began fighting among themselves for preeminence. Whoever controlled William would have an obvious advantage, so for the next few years the young duke was treated as a pawn and moved around to whichever guardian was momentarily dominant.

While William's entourage was distracted, unrest spread. Thanks to all the new castles it became effectively impossible for a central authority to gain control, and even minor knights began to make power grabs of their own, carving out virtually independent principalities. Even worse, they also started to involve themselves in the game of capturing, and thereby controlling, William.

Throughout the decade, the boy was constantly on the move, hustled by a shrinking number of guardians from one stronghold to the next in a desperate bid to stay ahead of the assassin's blades. Relentlessly the noose drew tighter. The young duke's tutor was cut down on his way home and several advisors were pulled from their saddles and butchered. William's most powerful protector, Osbern fitz Arfast (Osbern the son of Arfast), known as the 'Peacemaker' for his diplomatic abilities, took the precaution of sleeping in his ward's bed, but even this wasn't enough. An assassin managed to slip past the guards and slit Osbern's throat right in front of his horrified charge.

Two other guardians, Count Gilbert and Count Alan, managed to hold things together, but in 1040 Gilbert was killed while besieging a rebel castle and the following year both Alan and William's tutor were assassinated.

What ultimately spared William was the realization by the nobility that a destabilized Normandy was to their advantage. A weak duke was harmless enough and infinitely preferable to the strong personality that would inevitably seize power in the event of an assassination. What the nobility really wanted was to be left to their own devices, and the illegitimate and youthful William could hardly interfere in their affairs. Far better to keep him scared and running, and then do what they pleased.

The bishop, Yves II of Belleme, an odious man who had recently killed his own wife to marry a more distinguished candidate, set the tone by carving out an independent domain within the borders of the duchy. When some political enemies were rash enough to enter his territory he chased them into a nearby cathedral and tried to force his way in. Since the doors proved too stout for his knights, he burned it to the ground with everyone still trapped inside. The fact that such behavior was inappropriate for a bishop – even one as secular as Yves – never seemed to have crossed his mind. The Lord of Belleme, like so many of his fellow nobles, would tolerate no challenge to his authority.

By now all vestiges of central authority had disappeared. Whoever controlled the local castle controlled the surrounding area, and the chaos started to attract the attention of predatory neighbors. The duke of Brittany, a cousin of William's, announced that before Robert had left for Jerusalem he had entrusted his son to Brittany's care – a patently false claim that he couldn't prove and that no one believed. Probably expecting this reaction, the duke invaded, but died just after crossing the border and the threat vanished. A more serious attack, however, soon followed. King Henry I of France, known to his contemporaries as 'Henry the Castle-grabber' was trying to gain control of the Seine Valley. Chasing an enemy over the border into Normandy, he demanded that a Norman castle be immediately turned over to him as an advance base. When the frightened guardians of William complied, the king demolished the fortress, and then rebuilt it to his own specifications in a successful bit of saber rattling.

The entrance of the king triggered a revolt. Many of the nobles, tired of rapacious ducal relatives and guardians, flocked to the king's banner in the hope that he would provide a more effective overlord. Even Falaise, the duke's birthplace, was seized by the rebels and fortified for the king.

With the situation growing more desperate by the hour, the one figure that no one had heard from, or expected to, abruptly made his appearance. William was fifteen years old, a man by the standards of the time, and ready to assert himself. Rallying his guardians, he chased the rebels out of Falaise, and led a spirited defense against the main conspirators. King Henry, sensing the wavering loyalty of the Normans, and in any case not prepared for a long engagement, withdrew, claiming that he had demonstrated his power and proved his point.

It's not surprising that William would finally emerge as a formidable personality. He must have had reserves of strength to survive such a childhood, and he had little patience for the fractious guardians who had held the reigns of power for him. Dismissing them en masse he surrounded himself with new advisors, mostly young and talented individuals who would stay with him for the rest of his life and become some of the largest landowners in England.

William, however, was playing a dangerous game. Most of the dismissed counselors were members of the ducal family, and they found it impossible to endure both the loss of their prestige and the humiliation of watching 'new men' get promoted over their heads. Some of them had as good a claim to the throne as William and an idea began to form that perhaps he could be removed after all.

At first they tried to respectfully petition that they be restored to their posts, but when William continued to show unmistakable signs of independent thought, they realized that the ground was shifting. For Yves II and his ilk there was only one course of action now available: the duke had to die.

An abortive assassination attempt was made in 1045, largely failing through the disorganization of its members, but this only served to increase their determination. Choosing Guy of Burgundy, an older cousin of William as ringleader, they made further plans to assassinate William. Speed was of the essence. By 1046 William was nearly eighteen, and they could feel their chances slipping away. When William left for a hunting trip in western Normandy, the conspirators made a solemn vow to murder him when he returned to the lodge for the night.

Fortunately for William, a jester overheard the conversation and warned the duke not to return home. Wary of his companions, William immediately fled, avoiding main roads and towns, fording rivers where he could and plunging through forests at full speed. At Ryes he met a friendly local lord who gave him a fresh horse and his three sons as an escort, and the four of them managed to make it safely to Falaise where he took refuge in the castle.

With half the duchy in revolt, William didn't know whom he could trust, so in desperation he appealed to his feudal overlord, King Henry the 'Castle-grabber'. This surprising decision turned out to be a shrewd move. The history between the two men was not so important as alliances shifted quickly in feudal Europe. A king was only as strong as his control over his vassals, and Henry had good reasons to support William. A weak duke propped up by royal power was infinitely preferable to a strong candidate like Guy of Burgundy, so he marshaled his army and joined William in Falaise.

The combined army met the rebels at the plain of Val-es-Dunes and risked everything in a pitched battle. Even with several defections, the rebels had numbers on their side, but they lacked coordination as Guy failed to impose himself and each noble disposed of his forces as he saw fit. An early skirmish managed to knock the king off his horse, but the royal forces rallied and after several hours of fighting the rebel army broke apart and was slaughtered as it tried to flee across a nearby river[1].

Although Guy of Burgundy managed to escape to the castle of Brionne and hold out for a few years, the revolt was effectively finished. The lesser nobility was exiled, and the more important ones were pardoned and returned chastened to court. William, for his part, wanted to make good use of the victory and moved quickly to consolidate his power. Oaths could be a potent force in medieval Europe and William – perhaps motivated by the dim memories of his father's Christmas ceremony – held a great 'peace council' near the site of his victory. It was an open-air meeting where the banks of the River Orne, so recently choked with rebel bodies, served as a potent reminder of the duke's power, and William invested the full weight of his office in the proceedings. Monks solemnly processed carrying precious relics belonging to a nearby abbey, and the assembled nobility swore to respect the peace.

It was a momentous achievement, and to commemorate it William built a little chapel on the site dedicated to peace.

The young duke had good reason to be proud. Still only twenty years old he had survived his childhood and against the odds had become a force to be reckoned with. The lawlessness and infighting had not quite ended – some still saw him as a pawn to be controlled – but he had taken great strides to stabilize the duchy. Now for the first time, his thoughts began to turn towards marriage to ensure the future of the dynasty.

Medieval marriages among the powerful were political matches chosen by others – feelings rarely if ever entered into the equation – but William had the rare luxury of independence. His father was dead, his mother wasn't in a position to influence anything and his advisors were either his age or had been discredited and removed. He was one of the few rulers of his time who got to choose his own wife, and he was determined to have it sanctioned by the Church to avoid the mistake of his father.

If William wanted to marry for love, he was also practical enough to make it politically advantageous for himself as well. After some searching, his eye settled on the beautiful[2] Matilda, daughter of his powerful neighbor the Count of Flanders and niece of the king of France. She would prove an inspired match. Nearly the same age as William, she was a formidable personality in her own right and they would apparently remain faithful to each other their whole lives. Uncharacteristically for a Norman duke, there would be no mistresses or illegitimate children.

Before they could get married, however, a potential problem arose. William and Matilda were fifth cousins and the Church forbade unions to the seventh degree. It was also discovered that Matilda's mother had been betrothed for a time to William's uncle and although the marriage hadn't been carried through, it was still seen as a violation of the accepted familial distance.

Such issues were common enough in the Middle Ages. Since marriages were usually contracted between members of the same class, the royal pool had become somewhat shallow;

nearly everyone was related to everyone else, and unless there were political reasons to object, most times a polite blind eye was turned.

Pope Leo IX, however, had a number of reasons to make life difficult for the Normans. As one of the first great reforming popes he believed that rulers should provide an example for the masses, and Normandy was notorious for the bad behavior of its clergy. Along with rampant simony – the practice of buying church offices – the worldly clerics often showed a complete disregard for their flocks. A steady stream of complaints about Norman abuses came to the attention of the pope, and he had reasons of his own not to ignore them.

For one thing he depended on the German[3] emperor, Henry III, for support, and Henry was currently quarreling with Matilda's father. More importantly – as far as Pope Leo was concerned – was the fact that the Norman mercenaries who had arrived in Italy were becoming quite a nuisance. Led by a ferocious pair of brothers named Humphrey and Robert Guiscard, they had so alarmed everyone with their growing power that Leo himself was about to personally lead a coalition army to chase them out of Italy. Therefore, when the request came from William for permission to marry Matilda, the pope responded by holding a council condemning simony instead – a clear message of his disapproval.

Not surprisingly, most of the Norman bishops skipped the event. They were almost certainly guilty and had no desire to face condemnation for their concubines and other indiscretions. Those that did attend returned to Normandy with the unwelcome news that the pope had specifically forbidden the marriage.

William went ahead anyway, and the next year married Matilda in a private ceremony. He didn't have long to wait for the political winds to change. The Norman brothers Humphrey and Robert smashed the pope's great army and took him captive. A year later Leo was dead and the next pope decided it was wise to make peace with Norman power. In exchange for a commitment to build two abbeys and several charitable institutions, William's marriage was officially sanctioned.

By that time William had other things on his mind. The Count of Anjou had moved into neighboring Maine and had seized some of its castles on the border. This threatened both Normandy and its neighbors, and King Henry, always wary of over-mighty vassals, arranged a joint expedition with William to check him. When William arrived, the inhabitants of an adjacent town made the poor decision to hang animal hides on the walls and beat them with sticks, chanting "the skin of the tanner belongs to his trade" – a less than subtle taunt about William's low birth and his mother's occupation. The furious duke responded by capturing thirty-two members of the garrison and having their hands and feet cut off in full view of the town. They promptly surrendered.

The whole campaign was just as short, and (if Norman sources are to be believed) William proved so gallant and masterful on his horse that even the Count of Anjou was impressed. At one point the Norman duke evicted a garrison by having two children sneak into a castle and set it on fire. This kind of resourcefulness, however, ultimately backfired. King Henry, unnerved by the speed at which William progressed, became convinced that his ally was now too powerful. Abruptly switching sides, he made an alliance with Anjou and wheeled around to crush the presumptive duke.

The royal treachery was particularly dangerous because it happened to coincide with yet another rebellion by two of William's uncles, so he resorted to a policy of falling back and biding his time. The king, finding no resistance and confident of success, divided his forces in half, sending one column under the command of his brother to Rouen, while he mopped up any resistance in the countryside. Unfortunately for the royal forces, however, the king's brother proved to be totally incompetent.

By the time he reached upper Normandy, the royal sibling had stopped making even the most preliminary nightly precautions. While bivouacking in the little village of Mortemer, his soldiers got their hands on the wine supplies and decided to sleep off its effects without bothering to post a guard. The Norman army fell on them in the middle of the night, leaving few survivors. William informed the king of the debacle by having an envoy climb a tree and shout news of it into Henry's camp. The king prudently withdrew and without his support the rebellion collapsed.

If anything, the abortive invasion had strengthened William. The duke was left in firm control of his domain with a burnished military reputation that cowed his vassals and made rebellion less likely. He could afford to be magnanimous in victory. Both of his rebellious uncles were exiled but they were given generous stipends as befitted sons of a duke.

King Henry, however, wasn't finished with William. He had clearly underestimated this dangerous young man, and needed to undermine his reputation before he grew too powerful. In 1057 he again allied with the Count of Anjou and marched into southern Normandy, determined to topple the duke from his throne. This time, the allies formed one army and headed for the coast.

With no rebellion to worry about William was in a much stronger position, but he didn't intend to risk his new credibility in a battle against a larger army. He was content to play his waiting game, refusing to engage the royal army until an opportunity presented itself. This tactic paid off once again. The king wasn't knowledgeable about local tides, and while he was crossing a marshy estuary, the rising water cut his army in half. William pounced, and the stranded soldiers panicked, many drowning in the sea. King and count were powerless, forced to watch impotently from the other side as the disaster unfolded.

The defeat dealt a serious blow to the king's prestige, and although he managed to extricate himself from Normandy, he was never the same again. Three years later, both king and count were dead and the political situation of France had changed drastically. The new king was only eight and the Count of Anjou died childless. Two of the count's nephews started a civil war to seize power, a state of affairs that the crafty William did his best to prolong. For the first time in his life Duke William was free from external threats.

Normandy had never been more confident. Despite the unrest, the duchy was richer than its neighbors, and distinguished immigrants began to wander in. Lanfranc, a celebrated teacher from Pavia, brought a young St Anselm, helping to start a literary revival that would soon spread to all of France. A large Jewish community settled in Rouen, making it a center of commerce, and a luxury wine trade began to flourish. The increased revenue trickled down to the nobility, who in turn built new abbeys and churches, further spreading the revival of learning.

William was now uniquely placed for the great opportunity of his life. Unchallenged at home or abroad, in his early thirties with a brimming treasury and a confident principality at his back, it must have seemed as if anything was within his grasp. Buoyant and self-assured, he turned his eyes towards the rich kingdom across the Channel.

Chapter Six

THE ANGLO-SAXON KINGDOM

England was a ripe fruit waiting to be plucked. King Edward the Confessor, now in his early sixties and in poor health, had no children of his own, and wasn't expected to last much longer. Even better for William, the old king clearly had Norman sympathies and had surrounded himself whenever he could with Norman advisors, appointing Frenchmen to at least three bishoprics and an earldom. Although twenty years older than the duke, Edward was William's first cousin and had spent a long exile in Normandy establishing close ties with the ducal family. The two men were probably reasonably close, and Edward may even have held out the suggestion that William should be his heir[1]. The duke of Normandy, however, was not the only claimant to the English throne in 1066.

Real power in England had been held for a long time not by the king, but by the family of a remarkable figure named Godwin. His origins are unknown – he seems to have deliberately kept them vague – and he first appeared during the crisis that occurred when Edward the Confessor's father Ethelred the Unready was expelled from England. The Viking king, Cnut, invaded, and in the ensuing struggle Godwin chose to back the Anglo-Saxon resistance. This should have spelled the end of his career, but the wily Englishman won over Cnut by arguing that his stubborn opposition really proved his loyalty. After all, the prominent men of England had sworn an oath to be faithful to their native king and yet most of them had deserted to Cnut at the first sign of trouble. Who was to say that they wouldn't do the same to their new king? Godwin, on the other hand, stuck by the oaths he gave.

Impressed either by the reasoning or by the man, Cnut made Godwin the Earl of Wessex and kept him as an advisor, even taking him on trips back to Denmark. When Cnut died in 1035, Godwin, now one of the most powerful men of the kingdom, remained in place, advising both of Cnut's sons as they reigned in succession. It was during this period that he first became involved with Edward the Confessor.

Edward and his brother Alfred were living in Normandy, as they had been since their father's exile and the fact that two possible rivals for the throne were alive and well across the Channel annoyed Cnut's son Harold Harefoot. A letter was dispatched inviting the exiled princes back to England, hinting that some accommodation might be made to share power. Edward seems to have run into trouble raising a suitable escort, but Alfred immediately went to England where he was promptly arrested by some of Godwin's men. Godwin was in the delicate position of having the fate of the rebellion in his hands. If he chose to back Alfred's bid, he would probably be handsomely rewarded by the new administration. On the other hand, he already enjoyed significant power and prestige and it made little sense to risk it all in favor of a naïve, unseasoned exile. So Godwin dutifully turned Alfred over to the authorities where he was blinded so viciously that he died.

It may have been the correct political move, but the murder outraged popular opinion and stained Godwin's reputation for the rest of his life. He protested his innocence in the affair, pointing out rather disingenuously that he hadn't carried out the deed himself, but was never able to clear his name. This emerged as a significant problem, because Viking rule of England proved unexpectedly short. Harold Harefoot died of disease within five years of taking the throne and his brother expired somewhat more memorably as he was rising to toast the bride and groom at a wedding feast.

This left the king of Denmark as the closest male heir, but the English had grown tired of Viking rule and began to look for a return of the native dynasty. Godwin, ever the political survivor, threw his support to the unlikely Edward, still exiled in Normandy. It was a shrewd move. The new king was in his late thirties, with a weak personality that was easily dominated, and the ambitious Godwin had big plans. There were six great earldoms in England and he had six sons that he intended to make earls. Even more promising was the fact that Edward was still a bachelor, and Godwin happened to have an available daughter. If he couldn't gain the throne himself, he could at least co-found a dynasty.

For the first few years everything went according to plan. His daughter became queen, two-thirds of the land in England fell into his family's control, and two of his sons were made powerful Earls. What he hadn't counted on was the king's smoldering hatred of an overbearing counselor – especially one who had had a very public hand in the death of a close family member.

Edward also had other reasons to resent Godwin. Wherever he looked, he found a member of the detested family. They were hanging around his palaces, in his council rooms, even in his bed. He was too weak to rule without them, but he struck back where he could. When Godwin's eldest son Svein, the black sheep of the family, kidnapped and raped a nun, Edward seized the chance to openly criticize his powerful advisor. When the disgraced Svein ignored the censure and murdered his own cousin, the king exiled the young noble, despite Godwin's formal protests. Things got even worse for the earl the following year. One of the king's Norman advisors was involved in an incident in Dover that claimed the lives of several townsmen. Since Dover was in Godwin's territory, the king cleverly ordered him to punish the town. Realizing that they had been provoked, and sensing public sentiment running against Edward's foreign advisors, Godwin refused and gathered his army.

Tensions may have been high against the Normans at court, but for once the earl had badly misjudged the situation. Despite the mutual animosity, the practical English were not willing to risk civil war over a few unpopular Frenchmen, and when the king showed up with an army, Godwin's forces started to melt away. Shaken by his eroding support, the earl asked the king what he needed to do to restore the peace. Edward's answer must have terrified him. "Give me my brother Alfred back," he reportedly said.

Godwin took the only course available to him and fled the country with most of his wealth – which by this time nearly rivaled that of the king. Despite this setback, the earl had a number of things working in his favor. The king may have had momentum on his side but that couldn't last forever, and Godwin had powerful allies in the country working for reconciliation.

The most important factor, however, was the king himself. Edward wasn't built for confrontation. He would often fly into a rage, but when it passed he would subside into meekness and more often than not pardon everyone. He was far too weak to hold his ground; sooner or later Godwin would be back.

As it turned out, the exile only lasted a year. While Godwin took refuge in Flanders, his capable son Harold traveled to the family estates in Ireland to raise additional support. The two of them then jointly sailed to England where they were greeted as heroes as they landed on the coast. Public resentment against Norman influence at court had risen again, and men flocked to Godwin's banner. Once again the two sides armed themselves – with Godwin loudly protesting his innocence – but this time momentum was against the king. His summons to gather his forces were largely ignored, and it became obvious that he would have to come to terms with the earl.

Godwin handed over two hostages – a son and a grandson – and again swore that he was innocent of Alfred's murder. In return, the king begrudgingly announced that he was restored to full favor. The only thing that marred Godwin's triumph was the fate of the hostages. They were given to a Norman archbishop for safekeeping, but due to the anti-French mood prevalent at court, he fled to Normandy taking the boys with him. There they were seized by Duke William who immediately announced that they had been given to him to support his claim to the throne. At that moment, however, the threat appeared to be remote and he was largely ignored.

The stress of this latest campaign took its toll on Godwin, and his health began to rapidly decline. At the Easter court the next year he suffered a stroke and, after a short period of incapacity, the sixty-year-old earl died[2].

Fortunately for the family, there were still four sons of Godwin in the country, the eldest of whom – Harold – easily stepped into his father's shoes. Under his smooth handling, tensions at court subsided. The new earl was in his early forties, tall, handsome, and most importantly, too young to be implicated in Alfred's murder. His main character trait seems to have been an easy-going bonhomie and an ability to put people at ease. According to a biography written in his lifetime, he "could bear contradiction well and never retaliated for it" – a quality rare in men of power at any age.

Harold was too subtle to roughly dominate the king the way Godwin had. Instead he seems to have used his considerable charisma to apologize for Edward's frequent outbursts, placating offended nobles or neighbors, and soothing the king's ruffled ego. Highly educated by eleventh-century standards, he owned a collection of books on falconry, probably knew French, Norse, Flemish, English, and some Latin, and founded and endowed a secular college at Waltham. He traveled widely and even made a pilgrimage to Rome, 'passing' as one contemporary wrote 'with watchful mockery through all ambushes as was his way'.

As Edward aged, he turned the daily running of the government over to Harold so he could concentrate on the great building project of his reign – Westminster Abbey. Harold's role in controlling the affairs of state was widely recognized by the population. He was commonly known as 'subregulus', literally 'under-king' or even 'Dei Gratia Dux' (Duke by the Grace of God), an appellation usually reserved for royalty. He proved to be a careful steward, far more vigorous in foreign affairs than Edward ever was, largely because he led with a firm hand. Unlike the king he was also an accomplished warrior who was willing to fight when he had to. He cut his teeth on the formidable Welsh Marches[3] and was rewarded for his prowess by the gift of the head of his most fearsome enemy as an offer of peace. Like any capable ruler, however, he knew the limitations of brute force. If possible he always preferred to come to terms without bloodshed. No less than three rebellions were settled by Harold without fighting – a tribute to his diplomatic finesse.

By 1057 it had become quite clear that Edward the

Confessor would never have children. Either because of a personal inclination or a physical impairment, the king probably never consummated his marriage to Godwin's daughter. It's been suggested that repudiating his daughter in this way was Edward's small attempt to defy Godwin, but the practical result was that the search for an heir had to begin. A surviving male relative of the royal family was found living in Hungary and a delegation was sent to retrieve him, but he died shortly after reaching England leaving only a five-year-old son named Edgar. The boy was clearly too young to inherit the kingdom, but the crisis seemed to have been averted. Edward only had to survive long enough for Edgar to become an adult.

With things seemingly in order, Harold fatefully left England for Normandy. Why exactly he did so isn't clear – the Bayeux Tapestry merely shows him getting into a ship without an explanation as to what he was doing. The Normans later claimed that he had come to confirm William's claim to the throne, while some English apologists advance the equally improbable scenario that he was on a fishing trip and got blown off course. A more likely motivation was that Harold was trying to secure the release of his brother and nephew who were still in captivity in Rouen. Regardless of the aim, however, the trip was a disaster. Caught in a storm off the Norman coast, Harold's ship was forced to land in the neighboring county of Ponthieu where he was seized by a local count and thrown into prison.

William could hardly believe his luck. His main rival for the throne had quite literally fallen into his lap. The duke quickly forced the Count of Ponthieu to hand over Harold, escorted him to Rouen, and feted him in style. Then he personally presented Harold with arms and invited him to join in a campaign against neighboring Brittany. Harold showed his usual flair, impressing his hosts during the maneuvers –

the Bayeux Tapestry shows him hauling two Norman soldiers out of quicksand – but he can have had no illusion about the danger he was in. Despite the attention being lavished on him, he was a prisoner and everyone knew it. The moment they arrived back at Rouen, it became clear what William would demand in return for his release.

Harold was forced to swear that he would support William's claim to the throne and do everything in his power to see that William became the next king of England. After the ceremony Harold was released, and although he had to say goodbye to his brother – they would never see each other again – he could at least console himself with the presence of his nephew whom William had allowed to go free. Nevertheless, it was probably a gloomy trip back to England.

He arrived to find yet another crisis brewing. His younger brother Tostig had been appointed Earl of Northumbria, but had so mismanaged affairs that his annoyed subjects had broken into his home, stolen everything that wasn't nailed down and killed those too slow to escape, adding for good measure that if he showed his face in York again they would do the same to him. Tostig, who was hunting with the king at the time, was taken completely by surprise. Edward, who seems to have had a close personal relationship with Tostig, flew into his characteristic rage and immediately called out his army, but got only a lukewarm response. A military campaign clearly wasn't possible. Since Harold personally knew everyone involved, including the leading men of Northumbria, he was sent as an official emissary to deal with the rebels. There he was faced with a personal dilemma. The rebel leaders made it clear that under no circumstances would they accept Tostig back and wouldn't lay down their arms unless he was exiled. Harold either had to support his family and plunge the kingdom into civil war, or betray his brother and send him into exile.

After some deliberation, Harold chose the latter course. Tostig would have to be sacrificed for the good of the country and go into exile. The king was apoplectic, suffering the first of the seizures that would kill him, but there was nothing he could do. Tostig, who never forgave his brother, fled to Scotland[4] and tried to raise an army to invade Northumbria.

The English had no time to think of the disgraced earl, or worry about a threat from the north. Edward the Confessor was dying and an official successor had to be chosen. The leading men of England – the Witan – met in December of 1065 and desperately looked to the king for guidance. The trouble was that there was no obvious choice. Harold was the most popular candidate; he had carried the burden of government for the last decade and clearly had the qualities of a good king, but he had no royal blood. The boy Edgar, on the other hand, had the right pedigree, but they could not in good conscience turn over the kingdom to a child in such dangerous times. William of Normandy of course was shouting that he had a claim, but it was fairly weak, and in any case the Normans were terrifyingly alien. No member of the Witan seriously considered him.

Edward, vacillating to the end, refused to give any direction. He suffered another seizure on Christmas Eve, and although he rallied enough to attend the yearly celebrations, a few days later he was too sick to attend the consecration of his life-long project, Westminster. He slipped into a coma, but revived briefly on January 4th for long enough to speak. Taking Harold's hand he named him as his successor and begged him to look after his queen. The next day he was dead.

Harold was crowned the same day that Edward was buried, disregarding the scandalized protests of the Normans who branded him an oath-breaker. The English countered that a vow made under duress wasn't binding, although they admitted that Harold tended to 'give oaths too easily'.

The new king tried to defuse the situation by moving immediately to strengthen his position in the North. He issued coins bearing the single Latin word 'PAX', although ironically he would see little peace in his reign. Word arrived almost immediately that William of Normandy was raising a huge army and Harold summoned the 'fyrd', a public levy of all free men, to defend the coast.

As the spring turned into summer, however, no invasion fleet was seen on the horizon. Harold couldn't keep his militia assembled forever, they were only obliged to serve for a limited time, and most had to get back to the more important task of bringing in the harvest. Harold kept them as long as he could, but on September 8th, with provisions running out and men deserting daily, he officially disbanded the army.

Medieval armies didn't fight in the winter, and it was now too late in the campaigning season for a serious invasion as autumn storms made the Channel crossing especially treacherous. The king retired to London, but a week and a half later stunning news arrived. England had been invaded, but not from Normandy. Without warning, the terrifying Viking king Harald Hardrada had struck from the North – and with him was the traitor Tostig.

Chapter Seven

THE CONQUEST OF ENGLAND

The news that Tostig had reappeared – with an army of Vikings in tow – must have seemed almost too sensational to be true. It probably even surprised Tostig himself. During his exile he had made appeals to several rulers for help but had been turned away at every turn with humiliating regularity. Finally, desperate and alone, he sailed to Norway and somehow gained an audience with its king, Harald Hardrada.

The old Viking needed no convincing to look for a battle. He was a unique figure, even by the standards of his time. Fifty years old in 1066, he had been first wounded in battle three and a half decades earlier and showed no signs of slowing down. The name 'Hardrada' can be roughly translated as 'hard-bargainer', and those who didn't respect his cunning usually ended up on the receiving end of one of his famous ruses. Norse poets were already singing of his exploits in his lifetime. Enormously tall with large hands, a booming voice, and a reddish blonde beard, he appeared every inch a Viking king. His personal banner was a snowy white field with a single black raven appropriately named the 'Landwaster', and although nominally a Christian (his half-brother would become the patron saint of Norway) he nevertheless had two wives and led a life dedicated to the twin goals of fighting and hoarding gold.

At the age of fifteen he entered the losing side of a battle and had to hide in the forests until his wounds healed enough for him to travel. Limping his way into Russia, he spent one year in the service of the Prince of Novgorod, where he fell in love with his employer's daughter. Asking for her hand in marriage, he was rejected because he had no throne or wealth, so he left for Constantinople to remedy the situation. There were plenty of opportunities in the Queen of Cities for an ambitious Viking. The empress Zoë, daughter of the last great Macedonian emperor[1], offered him service in the famed Varangian Guard, the elite corps of Scandinavian mercenaries that provided the empire's best troops. The energetic Hardrada quickly rose to become Captain of the Guard, spending his time sacking and raiding in North Africa and Sicily.

It was there that he first gained a reputation for cunning. While unsuccessfully besieging a town in Sicily he noticed birds nesting in the thatch of houses and flying out by day to the woods to find food. Ordering his men to catch the birds, Harald tied chips of wood to them, set them on fire and released them. The panicked birds flew to their nests, setting the town on fire. During another siege he fell sick, and while recuperating he decided to stage his own funeral. His men dressed themselves in mourning clothes and begged for a Christian burial within the walls of the city. The townsmen foolishly agreed, arguing – so we are told – about who would get the rich gifts the Norsemen were sure to leave with the body. The moment Harald's men were in the town, they dropped the coffin, blew a war blast for the rest of the army concealed nearby, and slaughtered everyone.

After a decade of fighting for the empire, Harald had amassed more wealth than any other Viking before him and decided that the time had come to go claim his Russian bride.

He had already sent most of his plunder to Novgorod for safekeeping and after concluding affairs in Constantinople[2] he collected his treasure and new wife and returned to Norway.

Hardrada's nephew was ruling the country at the time, so Harald started a civil war to elbow him aside. The nephew magnanimously offered to split the kingdom to prevent further bloodshed, and five years later he conveniently died, leaving Harald as the sole king. This may have satisfied any other man, but after a summer or two without fighting, he decided that he should be king of Denmark as well. The Danes were perfectly happy with the king they had, however, and resisted him with a stubbornness that matched his own. After fifteen summers spent fruitlessly trying to ravage his way to the throne, Harald realized he was getting nowhere and made a rare truce. Two years later Tostig arrived, dangling the wild promise of the English throne in front of him, and the bored Hardrada jumped at the chance. Calling for his army, he boarded his longship, the Dragon, and set sail for England.

On the Tuesday after Easter a 'hairy' star – Halley's Comet – had been seen in the sky and this was widely interpreted as an ill omen. Now, just weeks after its disappearance the Norse arrived and seemed to confirm everyone's worst fears. The teenaged northern earls, Edwin and Morcar, had never fought a battle before, but they gathered the local levee and met the invaders at Fulford, a mile outside the city gates of York. The fighting lasted less than an hour, but it was a disaster for the English. Harald's beserkers tore into the Anglo-Saxon lines, driving them into a nearby marsh where Norse poets claimed that so many were killed that the Vikings could cross it on English corpses and keep their feet dry.

The battle effectively sealed York's fate, and the city

immediately surrendered to prevent further slaughter. Harald and Tostig, who seemed to believe that they had conquered the entire north of England at a blow, demanded five hundred hostages. Since it would take time to round them up, Harald agreed to give York four days to find them, stipulating that the hostages should be brought to Stamford Bridge, seven miles east of York. With that accomplished they returned to their ships and spent the following days drinking and feasting.

The ships were moored fourteen miles from Stamford Bridge, and when the appointed day came, it was warm, so most of Harald's soldiers left their mail shirts behind and leisurely made their way to the site. When they saw a cloud of dust approaching from York they assumed it was their prisoners, but as it approached Harald saw weapons 'shimmering like ice'. Tostig, deluded to the end, assured him that it was probably his kinsmen coming to pledge their support, but it soon became clear that it was nothing of the sort.

King Harold of England had been in London when he heard of the Norse invasion and he had managed to accomplish one of the most extraordinary military feats of Anglo-Saxon England. Assembling his elite housecarls he immediately started riding, gathering more recruits as he went, both day and night, covering the two hundred miles in an astonishing four days. Entering York before anyone knew he had even left London, he posted guards on every major road so no news of his arrival would leak out.

The next day he rode out to confront his enemies. Trying as always to come to terms peacefully, he asked his brother if he would lay down his arms in exchange for his old earldom. "And what will you give my ally, Hardrada?" Tostig asked. "Six feet of English soil," was the reply, "or since he is a tall man, a little more."

Hardrada should have retreated to his ships where he had fresh reserves, but his blood was up, and after sending three runners to get the men from the longboats, he went roaring into the attack, wildly swinging a battle axe with each hand. Even with his forces half-armed, Hardrada was a formidable foe and the battle lasted most of the day. By the time the men from the ships arrived Hardrada was dead, hit in the throat with an arrow, but the survivors grimly fought-on refusing to surrender, some even throwing off their armor and giving in to a berserker rage.

When night fell there was hardly a Viking left alive on the field. The next day Hardrada's son, Olav, came and asked for mercy, and Harold wearily let him go after a promise never to return again. The Hard-Bargainer had come to England with two hundred and forty ships, but only twenty-four were needed to carry the survivors back to Norway.

There was little time to savor the victory. A week was spent sorting out the situation in York where the easy capitulation to the Vikings had inspired bitter feelings among those who had wanted to resist. Harold held a great feast to sooth tensions, but in the middle of it a messenger burst in to announce that the Normans had landed at Pevensey, on the south coast of England.

William's invasion, although minutely planned, had run into a string of problems. He had raised an impressive force from all over France, and built a fleet of Viking style ships that supposedly numbered nearly seven hundred. Men and material flowed to the meeting point, but delays kept bogging the endeavour down. The weather refused to cooperate, preventing the intended late-summer crossing, and wrecking several ships with sudden squalls. On top of that, William faced the same problem that had caused Harold to disband his army: Normandy's feudal forces were only obligated to appear for forty days; after that they had to be paid like everyone else, and the cost was growing prohibitive. The longer William had to wait, the more people doubted his chances of success. In mid-September, with his ships still moored to the coast, and seemingly endless rain and fog, the entire project threatened to descend into farce.

Then on the 27th of September the weather unexpectedly cleared. William boarded his magnificent flagship the *Mora* – a gift from his wife – and cast off at once. The night crossing was relatively calm. Early the next morning the lookout caught sight of the massive walls of the old Roman fort of Pevensey, and William's soldiers disembarked without incident. Remarkably, the long delays had worked in the duke's favor. Had they arrived at the beginning of August as William intended, they would have come face to face with the English army. Now, however, they were unopposed and since a medieval army's options were to move or starve, they ravaged their way towards Hastings.

Two hundred miles away, Harold was already on the move. Repeating his epic march, he was back in London within four days to plan the defense of the realm. But the king was very near emotional and physical exhaustion. Of the last two weeks, eight days had been spent in hard riding, one full one in a bruising battle, and the remaining five in desperate diplomacy. It was only now, fatigued and vulnerable, that he got word that William had brought with him both the relics that Harold had sworn on in Normandy, and a papal bull of excommunication giving the pope's blessing to William's invasion.

It was a devastating blow, a vivid reminder of Harold's broken oath and horrible confirmation that God's judgment had gone against him. Harold's brother, Gyrth, begged him to stay behind and not risk battle, pointing out that if Harold died all was lost. He further suggested that he would take his brother's place, since he was expendable; Harold could stay behind and gather more men while stripping the country of supplies. If fighting didn't overcome William, starvation surely would. This was a sensible, even a brilliant plan, but Harold rejected it out of hand and on October 14th he assembled his men on a narrow ridge overlooking the field of Hastings.

William's plan of battle was relatively simple. Since the English fought on foot in their traditional shield-wall, he would soften up the line with arrows, then send in the infantry. When the English line showed signs of wavering he would order a cavalry charge to finish them off. However, when he put this plan into action, the shield-wall unexpectedly held. When the knights came storming up the hill they met the English housecarls, elite forces who fought with huge battle-axes, and after sustaining horrendous wounds it was the knights who broke and fell back. Some of the English, seeing their opponents scatter, ran down after them, and had the whole army followed the battle may have ended there. A rumor started that William had been killed, and the Normans started to panic. But William, who was alive and well, lifted his helmet to show that he was unharmed and led a rally, trapping and slaughtering the English who had come racing down the hill.

As the day wore on the battle became one of attrition. Norman arrows and cavalry charges began to take their toll, depleting the English line, and it gradually began to shrink in on itself. Both sides began to suffer setbacks. Harold's brothers, Gyrth and Leofwine, were killed as they commanded opposite wings of the army, and William had three horses killed underneath him. The Norman archers began to angle their arrows up over the shield-wall so they fell on the unsuspecting men behind, and – if we are to believe the usual account – in the late afternoon one of these struck Harold in the eye. As the king lay in agonizing pain from this dreadful wound, a group of four Norman knights burst through and hacked him apart.

When Harold's standard fell the end came quickly. Some English made a last stand in the woods, killing many pursuing Normans in the gathering dark, but most simply fled. William called off any longer pursuit and began to search for Harold's body, identifying it the next day with the help of Harold's mistress. He had the body washed, and according to legend, wrapped it in a purple shroud and buried it under a pile of stones overlooking the coast with an epitaph that read "By command of the Duke, you rest here a king, O Harold, that you may be still guardian of the shore and sea".

It's been famously said that William overthrew the strength of England in a single day, but that isn't quite true. He had won an important battle and killed his rival, but he was still in a very precarious position. As far as he knew there were huge native armies gathering against him, while he was isolated in the middle of a hostile country with limited supplies and no reinforcements. He was also running short of wine – a serious problem since the local water had given his men such severe stomach flu that several died from it. In London, meanwhile, the young Edgar was elected king and the secular nobility there swore to fight for him.

Unfortunately for the English, however, there was a conspicuous absence of leaders, and virtually no one of standing above the age of twenty. The boy king couldn't inspire much effective leadership, and by the time William arrived in London with his army the will to fight was gone. The gates were opened and William entered in triumph. His coronation was marred somewhat by his soldiers who mistook the shouts of acclamation for the beginnings of a riot and set fire to the city, but he received the customary oaths of loyalty from the assembled populace and nobility and he swore to be a good king.

William no doubt hoped to rule a willing, peaceful people, but he would have little peace in his reign. Harold's sons tried several times to invade from Ireland; the boy king, Edgar, fled to Scotland and stirred up trouble to the north; and freedom fighters like the legendary Hereward the Wake repeatedly tried to throw off the Norman yoke. It took five years of ruthless oppression to bring the north of England under his control, and few years passed after that without some disturbance. In 1083 his wife Matilda died, removing a moderating influence on him, and William grew increasingly tyrannical. He did make a number of significant reforms, most important of which was the Domesday Book – a vast accounting of what everything in the kingdom was worth. But William never liked the people or the countryside of his adopted country. He never bothered to learn the language, and his habit of rewarding land to followers had the effect of alienating his subjects. To the English he remained a cruel and foreign tyrant for his entire life, best symbolized by the massive structure he built in London – the White Tower – heart of the Tower of London.

William spent as much time as he dared at home in Normandy, and it was there that he died in 1087. He had been besieging a castle when his horse suddenly reared, throwing him against the pommel of his saddle and fatally rupturing his stomach. After pardoning his political enemies, the fifty-nine-year-old monarch died, splitting his kingdom among his three sons. Tellingly, to his oldest, Robert, he gave his favorite part, the Duchy of Normandy; to his second, William Rufus, he gave the throne of England; and to his youngest, Henry, he gave about 5,000 pounds of silver.

His corpse, too fat to fit into the coffin and left unattended for a few days while his sons squabbled for their inheritance, burst when it was forced into the crypt, and was buried as quickly as possible with little ceremony. His stunning conquest of England – the last time a foreign invasion successfully conquered the country – tied England to the Continent and in the long run proved a great benefit to both Europe and the West. But none of that was any comfort to those who had had to go through it.

Within twenty years of the conquest it's been estimated that two hundred thousand French and Normans settled in England, and one in five of the native population were either killed or starved by the seizure of farm stock or land. French replaced English as the court language and nearly every major Anglo-Saxon figure disappeared. The English were forced to watch as their leaders were reduced to poverty, thrown into dungeons, mutilated or killed. Heavy taxes were imposed, huge swaths of the country were depopulated to act as royal hunting forests, and vindictive laws were passed to the disadvantage of the natives. Most hated of all were the castles that William had built all over England, visible symbols of their oppression which were constructed and paid for with English labor and wealth.

The conquest of England also had another legacy. The ruler of Normandy had always been a vassal of the French king, and the addition of England didn't change that. Now the English king would have to perform the ceremonial acts of homage for the lands of Normandy, something that no British sovereign was ever going to do. For the moment the French monarchy was weak, but when it eventually asserted itself it would spark a century-long war to evict the English from France.

As for King Harold, the English began to look back on his

brief reign with longing and inevitably a legend started that he had survived Hastings and lived out his life as a monk. His family, as can be expected, suffered horrendously at Norman hands. They had been among the most wealthy and prominent before the Conquest, but after it they rapidly disappeared. Harold's sons and brothers were hunted down and either killed or imprisoned, and his wife and daughters were scattered in exile. Harold's daughter, Gytha, fled to western Russia where she married the Grand Prince of Kiev. Their granddaughter married a Danish prince and gave birth to a son who became the king of Denmark. One of that king's descendants is Queen Elizabeth II of Great Britain. Fittingly enough, the royal family now has the mingled blood of both Harold and William.

As a final post-script, Great Britain erected a monument in Bayeux to the soldiers who had died storming Normandy's beaches in World War Two. Beneath it they left a plaque which reads "We, once conquered by William, have now set free the Conqueror's native land".

Chapter Eight

BRAS DE FER

The conquest of England profoundly changed Normandy. The old, chaotic days had been receding for nearly a generation – with the exception of William's childhood – and the price of stability was the mass exodus of a good number of the duchy's younger sons. The minor nobility that was used to having things its own way soon discovered that life under a strong duke meant much less freedom, opportunity and power. As personal castles were torn down and the power of local strongmen evaporated, more and more of them began to look for opportunities abroad.

The eleventh century would prove to be the great period of Norman adventure, and although it was already half over by the time William the Conqueror first entered London, its greatest conquests still lay ahead. Remarkably enough they would largely be the achievement of a single family – not a noble or wealthy one, but that of a simple knight named Tancred de Hauteville. He was a second-generation Norman whose grandfather had arrived with Rollo, and he settled in southern Normandy on a small plot of land. Virtually nothing is known about him other than the fact that he was remarkably fertile. In addition to an unknown number of daughters, he had five surviving sons by his first wife, and another seven by his second. This was a problem since the family was relatively poor; once they came of age there was not nearly enough of an inheritance to go around.

Traditionally there were only two ways to resolve the issue. The boys could either divide the inheritance twelve ways making it too small to support anyone, or they could slug it out and let the victor claim the entire thing. Fortunately for the younger sons, at this point an uncle returning from pilgrimage in Italy advised them to try their luck there.

The first Normans had arrived in the peninsula as pilgrims at the beginning of the century. On their way to Jerusalem they had paused in the little town of Monte Sant'Angelo. Perched on the slopes of a limestone massif jutting up from the rolling Italian countryside of Apulia, the town had always seemed a place of special importance. The ancient Romans set up a popular shrine to a son of the healing god, Asclepius, and legend had it that the mountain was also sacred to Chalcas, the great Greek seer of the Iliad. Thanks to a timely fifth-century appearance by the archangel Michael, the waning of paganism did nothing to dent this mystical aura and its reputation, if anything, continued to grow. By the eleventh century the cave where the angel emerged had become a major stop on the pilgrim route. Popes, kings, and saints all came calling, eager to share in the celestial mysteries, and the walls of the adjoining chapel were soon covered with the offerings of those who had been miraculously healed. Even the most powerful secular rulers felt the pull. The German emperor, Otto III, walked barefoot from Rome, while his less pious successor, Henry II, hid in the grotto overnight to see if there was any truth to the rumor that the Archangels Michael and Gabriel would appear at midnight to celebrate the mass.

The most fateful visitors, however, arrived in 1016. An unassuming group of forty Norman knights on their way back from the Holy Land stopped at the cave to pay their respects. Just after they had entered, a small man dressed in the Greek style of flowing robes approached them and begged for help. He was a Lombard by the name of Melus who had spent his life in the cause of Lombard freedom but had been driven into exile by the Byzantines. All he needed, he claimed, was a few sturdy mercenaries to force the cowardly Byzantines back and liberate his people. To his delight, the Normans at once agreed to help. They couldn't come to his assistance immediately of course – they had come as pilgrims and it was hardly appropriate to march off to war – but they promised to return within a year.

It wasn't the appeal to nobility or brotherhood that inspired the Normans. They had a low opinion of southerners in general and Lombards in particular. A short time before, they had witnessed a Saracen attack on Salerno and been astounded by the cowardice of the locals. As far as they were concerned the Italians were effeminate and soft, and firmly deserved their subservient status. Melus, however, knew his audience well enough to have added the inducements of money and land to his request, and it was this that fired their imaginations. Gazing at the sun-drenched Apulian countryside stretching out before them, they must have relished the chance to gain a foothold in this beautiful land.

The alliance with the Lombards was short lived. Even with Norman arms stiffening their forces, they were crushed by Byzantine armies in the first real clash. The battle was enough to prove the worth of Norman swords to the Byzantines, however, and they immediately hired them to quash the troublesome insurgents. Abandoning the cause of Lombard freedom as easily as they had picked it up, the Normans cheerfully set to work enforcing the imperial will.

The oldest Hauteville son, William, reached Italy around 1035, just as the last Lombard resistance was being mopped up. Within months of his arrival, the Byzantine emperor decided to conquer Sicily and put out a great call for mercenaries. William, along with three hundred of his fellow knights enlisted immediately.

Under the brilliant Macedonian dynasty of Byzantium, the empire had turned the tide against the caliphate and was engaged in a great push to clear the eastern Mediterranean of Muslim pirates. The Macedonian line had ended with the death of Basil the Bulgar-Slayer in 1025, but although the emperors who followed him were weak, the army Basil had created was still formidable and won a string of victories in Syria and along the Anatolian and North African coast. Now the imperial forces turned their attention to Sicily hoping to clear out the main pirate nest and win a rich land of grain, cotton, sugar, and fruit groves for the empire. The timing looked especially good. Civil war had erupted in Sicily, the aristocracy was divided, and central authority was collapsing. Additionally, a large part of the population was still Christian, and could be counted on to act as a fifth column.

To command the invasion, the emperor chose George Maniaces, the rising star of the Byzantine world. Charismatic, headstrong, and larger than life in nearly every respect, Maniaces had a reputation as imposing as his physique. Even the usually unflappable members of the imperial court seemed stunned in his presence. After reporting that the general was ten feet tall and had a roar that could frighten whole armies, the imperial historian Michael Psellus concluded by saying that "those who saw him for the first time discovered that every description was an understatement".

His rise was as meteoric as it was unexpected. A decade

before he had been the governor of Teluch, an obscure city in Asia Minor, and if not for an unfortunate imperial humiliation, would probably have remained so indefinitely. The hapless emperor, Romanus Argyrus, in an attempt to bolster his military reputation, marched to war against the caliphate, but as he was traveling through a pass just north of Teluch some Saracen cavalry ambushed him. Thanks to some quick thinking and a change of clothes the emperor managed to escape, but his army scattered in a panic. Loaded down with loot from the imperial baggage, the Saracens rode to Teluch and gleefully informed Maniaces of the debacle, adding for good measure that the emperor was dead and his army destroyed. Since night was falling they sportingly gave him until the next morning to surrender, promising dreadful retribution if he refused.

Maniaces showed every sign of panic, assuring the Saracens that at first light he would appear in their camp with every bit of treasure the city possessed. As a gesture of his good intentions, he sent along a large amount of food and drink for the victors to enjoy. The wine in particular had the intended effect as the Saracens were parched and in the mood to celebrate. Before long they were hopelessly drunk and Maniaces' soldiers slipped into their camp and butchered every last man. When the bloody work was done, the governor ordered the ears and nose cut off of each corpse, gathering the grisly trophies in a sack. The next morning he set out on horseback to find his fleeing sovereign, and after reporting his triumph he dumped out the contents of the bag. The delighted emperor promoted him on the spot.

Even brash young knights like William de Hauteville must have found the army Maniaces gathered in Sicily impressive. In addition to the usual mercenary forces of Italian adventurers and grumbling Lombards who had been pressed into service, the general had brought with him a company of fierce Bulgarians and some Varangians under the command of the already semi-legendary Norse hero Harald Hardrada.

At first the great army carried all before it. Messina was the first town to fall, followed by Troina and Rametta. Within the next two years a dozen major fortresses in the east, were taken with only Syracuse managing to hold out. There, a spirited defense by the local emir frustrated every attempt to force the city walls, and each unsuccessful effort weakened the morale of the besieging army. After one particularly dismal episode the gates opened and the emir suddenly galloped out at the head of his forces. The sortie caught the Byzantines by surprise and they fell back in a panic. The retreat threatened to turn into a rout until William, seeing the danger from another section of the walls, leapt into action. Making a sudden charge straight for the emir, he struck him with all the force he could muster. The blow nearly split the man in half and sent him crashing lifeless from his saddle. The demoralized Saracens fell back to the city, but they had little more fight left in them, and asked for terms.

William's sword stroke had delivered Syracuse to the Byzantines, but more importantly it had provided the foundation of the Hauteville reputation. From that day on he was known as William Bras de fer, 'Iron-arm', and became the undisputed leader of the Normans in the south. When he returned to the Italian peninsula it would be as the most renowned figure of his day, and he would arrive with the first stirrings of a larger Norman destiny. The days of simple mercenaries were passing. From now on the Normans would serve themselves.

This dawning consciousness of their worth came at a bad time for the Byzantines, for despite the victories, the campaign was starting to fall apart. The imperial court, as always suspicious of too successful a general, had started to slow the shipment of supplies. Pay for the mercenaries began to lapse and disputes arose over the division of the spoils. Things came to a head when the Normans sent a Lombard emissary to formally lodge a complaint with Maniaces. Characteristically, the hotheaded general saw this as a personal affront and had the man whipped and paraded through the camp. The frustrated Normans left the expedition, bitterly protesting their treatment.

Despite the way it had ended, William's Sicilian expedition had been a great success. He had learned a valuable lesson. Sicily was rich and disunited, and there were plenty of Christian allies to aid any invasion. That bit of information was filed away for a more opportune moment. When the time was right, the Hautevilles would make good use of it.

In the meantime, William began to show his strength. Rekindling his old Lombard sympathies, he encouraged a rebellion and invaded Apulia, the richest part of Byzantine Italy, with a mixed Lombard and Norman army. The town of Melfi opened its gates to the 'liberators', giving the Normans their first real foothold in Italy. Within a year William had extended his control to the surrounding territory, a string of prosperous trading and fishing towns that produced so much grain, olives, vegetables and fruit that it was known (then as now) as 'Fat Apulia'. The local Byzantine governor was provoked into instigating a battle, and the two sides met on the site of the ancient fields of Cannae.

For the superstitious in both armies, it was an ominous location. Twelve centuries earlier the Carthaginian general Hannibal had inflicted one of the most humiliating defeats in Roman history on this spot by completely wiping out a consular army. The citizens of Rome had been so terrified that they indulged in their last recorded acts of human sacrifice, burying two people alive in the Forum and throwing an infant into the Adriatic. The Normans, however, had also experienced a disaster here. Just two decades prior to this a Byzantine force had thrashed a combined Norman and Lombard army so thoroughly that only ten Norman knights had survived.

If William had any qualms about fighting in such a fateful locale he didn't show it, giving instead every appearance of confidence. This was mostly due to the fact that although his forces were heavily outnumbered, they no longer had to deal with the terrible Maniaces. The great general had been outmaneuvered by his enemies at court and been recalled in disgrace.

His troubles had started when a wealthy and well-connected Anatolian neighbor named Romanus Sclerus accused him of encroaching on his land. Maniaces, who had difficulty controlling his temper in the best of times, had forgotten himself enough to administer a savage beating to the patrician. When Romanus recovered he swore revenge and took full advantage of the general's absence to loot his house, burn his fields and, as a final insult, seduce his wife. He spent the next year undermining Maniaces' reputation at court, successfully persuading the emperor to recall him.

With Maniaces gone the Byzantines could field no competent general against the Normans, and William, with his usual exquisite timing knew he only needed to provoke a battle. When the Byzantines sent an emissary to his camp, William gave him a terrifying welcome. The poor man launched into a prepared speech when suddenly a Norman knight crept up and struck his horse in the forehead. The stunned animal instantly crumpled to the ground throwing its rider. As one group of soldiers grabbed the diplomat another seized the horse and threw it off a cliff. They then shook the petrified man to his feet, provided him with another mount and told him to stop wasting their time with words. "Go back to your emperor", they said, "and tell him the Normans are ready to fight."

Despite having only three hundred knights and twice that number of foot soldiers, the Normans were considered a serious enough threat to warrant the presence of the Varangian Guard, Byzantium's elite fighters. Despite this, the imperial forces were unable to stand up to the Norman heavy cavalry and most of their forces were drowned trying to cross a river in a bid to escape. Two months later the Byzantines tried again, this time with regiments from Asia and a large number of the returning Sicilian forces, but were again defeated.

The victories against the hated Byzantines gave William a tremendous amount of prestige that he used to spread a revolt throughout the remaining Byzantine territory.

Constantinople at last awoke to the seriousness of the situation and quickly sent the one man capable of turning the tide. That spring Maniaces returned to Italy to crush his former mercenary. He did so with alarming violence, swatting aside a Norman force and engaging in a savage campaign against all the towns that had wavered in their loyalty. Dissidents were crucified, women were raped, and children were buried up to their necks and left to die. The brutal tactics worked. Local support for the rebellion evaporated and the Normans were left dangerously exposed.

But Byzantium was no longer the force it had once been and, plagued by its conspiracy-ridden court, it destroyed itself. Maniaces met his end in a suitably grand fashion, nearly bringing the entire empire to its knees in the process. His old enemy Romanus Sclerus had arranged another humiliating recall, but this time had overstepped himself. He just couldn't resist the temptation to enjoy his enemy's discomfort first hand and traveled to Italy to deliver the imperial summons in person. Unfortunately for Sclerus, Maniaces didn't take the news gracefully. Seizing Sclerus, he had the man's ears nose and mouth stuffed with horse dung, and then slowly tortured him to death. Hurling curses at the man on Constantinople's throne, Maniaces declared himself emperor and marched on the capital. There was no general in the empire capable of stopping him, and by the time he reached Thessalonica he had all but taken the crown. Here, however, fate intervened. Riding out to a skirmish with loyal imperial troops he was killed by a chance spear throw and his army disintegrated. The surviving rebels were paraded backwards on mules in the Hippodrome[1] and the empire was spared further bloodshed.

With military options no longer viable to restore the situation in Italy, Constantinople turned to the tried and true method of bribery to weaken the rebellion. The main Lombard ringleaders were offered generous pensions to switch sides, which they eagerly accepted, and the Normans were left once again on their own.

Though they were still technically fighting for Lombard freedom, the Normans no longer trusted their allies and decided to elect their own leader. The trouble was that they all saw themselves as equals and found it hard to accept a superior authority. They did recognize the need for a united command in battle, but the same independent and ambitious streak that had led them to seek their fortunes in Italy made them virtually ungovernable. William was the military hero of the rebellions and was dutifully given the title 'Count of Apulia', but this was mostly wishful thinking as the Normans only controlled a small part of it, and William had little real authority over his fellow knights. He was the first among equals, able to rally them against common enemies, but little else.

This, however, was enough for William to establish himself as a powerful figure in the region. Marrying the niece of the Prince of Salerno, he gained entry into the Lombard nobility and accepted the prince as his feudal overlord. In response, the prince officially invested him with Apulia, which was divided among the twelve most powerful Normans. The town of Melfi, which they had first conquered, was to be held in common by all twelve as a sign of equality.

William had come a long way from the landless son of a poor knight. Under his loose leadership the Normans had been transformed from simple Byzantine and Lombard mercenaries to landed barons. As a sign of the changing fortunes, he made it clear that he intended to push his old Byzantine employers out of Italy. In 1045 he invaded Calabria but was sharply checked near the southern Italian port city of Taranto. It proved to be the last campaign of his career. The following year, as he was readying yet another expedition, he caught a fever and died.

His death left the Normans of the south at a crossroads. There was clearly great opportunity, but also the beginnings of a dangerous backlash. The Lombards, Byzantines, and even the pope were by now concerned by the growing power of the Normans and threatened by the change in the status quo. Even the native populations of Apulia, who had welcomed the Normans as liberators, now began to see them as oppressors. All it would take was a single spark to ignite this growing anti-Norman storm.

The former mercenaries seemed oblivious to the danger. Eager for individual gain, they were disunited and busy trying to squeeze every bit of plunder from their conquests. What they needed was a leader who was strong enough to enforce discipline and direct Norman energy into productive channels. Unknown to them, that leader arrived in Italy just months after William's death.

Chapter Nine

GUISCARD

Following William's death his younger brother Drogo was elected to his position of Count of Apulia while a third brother, Humphrey, was given some of William's former estates. Back in Normandy the seven sons who had stayed behind were watching these developments with considerable interest. These were the children of Tancred's second marriage and in 1047 the eldest of them, Robert, decided to join his half-brothers in Italy.

He arrived to a cool reception. Drogo didn't particularly like his father's second wife and detested her children, so he sent Robert off with a small band of followers to cut his teeth in a frontier fortress deep inside Byzantine Calabria, the heel of the Italian peninsula. The castle overlooked a coastal plain which held the picturesque ruins of the ancient city of Sybaris[1], but if Robert expected anything approaching luxury he was quickly disillusioned. The small, dank fortress was malaria-ridden and dark, languishing in a particularly sparse region of Italy. Calabria was much poorer than Apulia, with a heavily forested, mountainous interior and little land suitable for agriculture. The coastal regions had been desolated by centuries of malaria and Saracen raids, and since the local populations were thoroughly Hellenized they were more loyal to the Byzantines and less likely to welcome the Normans as deliverers.

To survive, Robert was forced to live off the land, which he managed to do with a combination of cunning and brutality. A favorite tactic was to set crops on fire and then charge money to extinguish it, a scheme which did not improve his popularity with the local populations. Before long he was being called 'Guiscard' and 'the crafty', and had acquired a reputation among the other Normans as someone to watch. He was shrewd enough to understand that a good leader should be feared by his enemies and loved by his allies. To this end he shared every hardship with his men, eating at the same campfire and sleeping on the same hard ground, but was also remarkably generous. Wealth for him was always a means and almost never an end to itself. When a visiting Norman bishop mentioned that he was building a cathedral back home, Robert, whose own resources were stretched, loaded him down with every bit of treasure he owned. The financial loss was more than compensated by the public relations gain. The cleric returned to Normandy and brought with him stories of the wealthy, generous knight of Calabria, and Robert, who was chronically short of men, was inundated with fresh recruits.

Before he had had a chance to expand his power, however, he was swept up into a larger conflict. When the Normans had first arrived in Italy they had been greeted as liberators by a Lombard population that was eager to escape the imperial tax collectors. As time when on, however, they had discovered that the rapacious Normans were a good deal worse than the Byzantines that they had replaced, brutally suppressing any sign of independence and squeezing their provinces for every drop of money. When Byzantine agents entered Apulia looking for a way to destabilize Norman control and neutralize the threat in Calabria, they found a very receptive audience.

A massive conspiracy was hatched to assassinate every major Norman in Italy and in 1051 it was carried out. Drogo was cut down as he entered his private chapel, and by nightfall all of Apulia was in uproar.

The surviving Normans, still not fully understanding how much public opinion had turned against them, responded by brutally ravaging the lands of anyone who was involved, thinking that they could restore the status quo with a display of strength. This was the final straw, and it provoked a response from the most powerful figure in Italy, Pope Leo IX.

The papal palace in Rome had been deluged for years with woeful tales of rape, murder, and robbery along the major routes of southern Italy, all begging for assistance against the footloose bands of Norman mercenaries who respected no law but that of the sword. Such concerns might normally have been better directed towards the local secular authority, but Leo was uniquely suited to lead the charge. Already renowned for holiness in an age of worldly pontiffs, he alone had the charisma and standing to pull together the scattered powers of Italy into a cohesive force. The blood and death of battle didn't shock him – as a bishop he had led the field armies of the German emperor, Conrad II, in a raid on northern Italy and saw no reason why his new position should bar another outing.

The pope had had experience with the Normans before. They were uncomfortably close to the Papal States[2], were notorious for their simony – a practice he was doing his best to stamp out – and had already proved so irritating that he had refused William the Conqueror's request for a marriage in order to humble them[3]. If something wasn't done to stop these lawless and uncontrollable Normans, they would begin to encroach on Vatican territory. If the pope couldn't find some way to bring them to heel, his reputation would suffer accordingly and he would face the real danger of being surrounded by a sea of Normans.

His first thought had been to awe the Normans into submission. He had traveled to southern Italy where he summoned Drogo de Hauteville before him. Dressed in the full robes of his office, the Holy Father had coolly ordered him to rein in his men. Drogo had seemed appropriately chastened, but a few months later he had been assassinated and southern Italy was plunged into chaos.

For Pope Leo, now was the perfect time for him to strike. The Normans were leaderless and frustrated, flailing in all directions, and nearly every non-Norman baron of southern Italy, from Abruzzo to Calabria, had risen up against them. But he had to act fast before tempers cooled. Writing to the Byzantine emperor, Constantine IX, Leo offered a joint alliance and then traveled to Germany to discuss matters with his cousin the western emperor. Having shorn up imperial support for the anti-Norman coalition, he raised an Italian army as quickly as possible and marched into Apulia, proclaiming that he would put an end to the 'Norman menace'.

News that an invading army was on the way – led by the Vicar of Christ himself – finally woke the Normans to the danger. A desperate call went out to every able-bodied man and Robert hurried back from Calabria. Under the circumstances everyone was willing to put aside their past differences, and the united Normans elected the blunt, soldierly Humphrey, the oldest surviving Hauteville, as their leader. His first action was to send a message to Leo asking for terms, but Leo was in no mood to hear an appeal. He had his enemies right where he wanted them and didn't intend to let them escape.

Humphrey and Robert held a hasty conference to decide

what to do. They were heavily outnumbered, and the fact that the pope was there in person unnerved them. But as bad as the situation was it would only grow worse if they delayed. A Byzantine army was heading down the coast and if it were allowed to link up with Leo, the odds would become too great. There was a serious food shortage; the local population had gathered up the harvest despite the fact that it was still green, and there was simply nothing to eat. If they didn't attack now they faced the threat of starvation.

With no realistic alternative, the Normans drew up by the Fortore River near the little town of Civitate and sent another emissary to the pope. This time, however, it was only a ruse, and in the middle of the negotiations they attacked. Leo's Lombard allies were caught by surprise and fled in a panic, and were soon joined by the bulk of the army. Only the pope's German regiment stood their ground against the Norman charge, but they were now outnumbered and were slaughtered to a man. The pope, dressed in distinctive flowing white robes, watched the entire debacle from a nearby hilltop with growing horror. When it became apparent that his forces were beaten he rode to a neighboring town and anxiously demanded sanctuary. The townsmen, however, were aware of what had just taken place and had no intention of offending the victors. The moment a Norman soldier rode up to the gates Leo was unceremoniously tossed out.

The pope suffered his defeat graciously, walking proudly out to meet his enemies, and those watching from the walls might have wondered just who had won the recent struggle. The Normans fell down before him, begging for forgiveness and swearing that they were faithful Christians. Some knelt to kiss his ring, and still others ran to fetch him a horse and some refreshment. When he had dined they escorted him to the town of Benevento – maintaining a respectful distance – and installed him in its finest apartments. Their courtesy never slipped an inch, but not all the deference in the world could hide the fact that Leo was now a captive, and the news quickly spread throughout Europe: the Vicar of Christ was a prisoner of the Normans.

Their victory was more complete than they knew. The pope was humiliated and broken, but even if he had wanted to mount another challenge he would have found it impossible. Just a few months after the battle, the churches of Rome and Constantinople suffered a serious break and the threat of a vast anti-Norman alliance vanished along with any hope of cooperation between the eastern and western halves of Christendom.

The only thing that threatened the Norman position now was tension between the brothers, which was rapidly mounting. Humphrey tolerated his younger sibling better than Drogo had, but his patience was wearing thin. Robert was enjoying himself in Apulia and had no intention of hurrying back to impoverished Calabria. Things came to a head at a banquet hosted by the elder brother. He accused Guiscard of dragging his feet, and the furious Robert was offended enough to draw his sword before being restrained by his friends. Feeling bitter and humiliated, he made his way back to Calabria, and began the work of expanding his influence.

Happily for him, he found the situation had greatly improved in his absence. Byzantine power in Italy was in the middle of a spectacular collapse; shrinking budgets and dithering rulers in Constantinople had left much of the local population feeling abandoned, and the garrisons left behind were demoralized and easily convinced to surrender. One town after another submitted to Guiscard, and those that resisted were either overwhelmed or fell prey to one of his famous ruses. In Otranto he managed to talk his way through the gates, and by the fall had seized Calabria's one productive agricultural region. Each success gave him a greater reputation, which in turn brought in more recruits that allowed more fortresses and more victories. By 1057 even Humphrey had to admit Robert's ability.

The elder Hauteville was dying of malaria and exhaustion, and was well aware that the Normans were in desperate need of a new type of leader. Their stubborn independence made their conquests unstable, and their harsh rule fueled the anti-Norman feeling among the populations they dominated. It was no longer enough to be a good soldier; leadership of the fractious Normans now required diplomacy, statesmanship and vision if they were ever to become more than petty barons. Humphrey was determined to leave his people in the hands of someone who saw a greater destiny for them, and there was only one serious candidate. Swallowing his pride, he summoned Robert and the two had a public reconciliation.

Not everyone was pleased with the selection, however, and Robert had to spend several months putting down various Norman barons who contested his election. For good measure he forced even the loyal nobles to re-swear allegiance to him, then returned to the toe of Italy to complete the conquest of Calabria. Here his youngest brother Roger joined him. Barely twenty-five, Roger had the same broad Hauteville shoulders and large frame, but was more easy-going than Robert. Where Guiscard was calculating, Roger was convivial, but that merely masked an iron-willed determination.

At first the two of them worked together well. They made a stab at Reggio which commanded the straits between Italy and Sicily, and Robert felt comfortable enough to leave the campaign in Roger's hands as he returned north to put down yet another rebellion. They were too similar, however, for the partnership to work for long. Perhaps recognizing the family ambition in his brother, Robert refused to grant him land or an independent source of income. Roger was eager to build up his wealth so he could marry, and his frustration turned to anger when Robert started slowing down the payments for his garrisons. When he formally complained, Guiscard dismissed his concerns, suggesting that his brother would benefit from the same rough conditions that he had had to suffer in his early days.

This kind of response only made things worse, and before long the animosity escalated into a full-blown war. Roger went on a rampage through his brother's Calabrian lands, burning crops, pillaging the countryside and kidnapping merchants for ransom. Not one to back down, Robert responded in kind, and the resulting devastation caused a famine that provoked a massive popular revolt. The scale of the rebellion caught the Normans completely by surprise and soon threatened to spread into Apulia. The alarmed brothers hastily patched up a truce, agreeing to share all further conquests equally.

Peace was restored just in time for Robert to receive a papal ambassador summoning him to Melfi for a personal meeting. When he asked what the pope wanted, the answer must have seemed too incredible to be true. It had been barely five years since a pontiff had led an army to crush the Normans, and now one of his successors was asking for an alliance.

The reason for the about-face in Vatican policy was the election of Nicholas II, a reforming cleric who wanted to end simony – the practice of buying church offices – and free the papacy from external control. The German emperor had traditionally been the pope's protector, but in practice that had usually meant that the pontiff was a German puppet. The only way for the pope to break free was to find a counterbalancing power and the closest one available was the Normans.

Nicholas called a synod to meet at Melfi, and there made the alliance official. Robert pledged his loyalty and promised to defend him against the emperor. In return the pope confirmed his right to hold the land he had already seized and gave him the suggestive title 'Duke of Apulia and Calabria as well as Sicily yet to be conquered'. The fact that he didn't actually control all of Calabria – or any of Sicily for that matter – hardly bothered Guiscard. The pope had given him the legitimacy to conquer everything he could and he didn't intend to waste the opportunity.

He spent the next year evicting the Byzantines from Italy, reducing the imperial holdings to the single city of Bari in the heel of the Italian peninsula. There they stubbornly resisted, clinging on to their ancestral homeland, and Guiscard was willing to let them be for the moment. He already had a more tempting target in mind – the rich fields of Sicily – and could wait for the rest of Italy to fall into his grasp. It must have been a heady feeling as he looked across the straits to the island just off the coast. The son of a minor lord of France had raised himself to the same level as his contemporary, Duke William of Normandy. There were now two Norman duchies at opposite ends of Europe, both planning to invade an island kingdom. Sicily was ripe for conquest and exerted an irresistible pull on Robert. Things had only become more chaotic since his eldest sibling, William Iron-Arm, had left, and the island was now divided between warring Arab and Berber factions. Even more promising, one of the Berber emirs had actually invited Robert to come, asking for his assistance in fending off his rivals. The two brothers crossed to Sicily in

1060 and immediately seized Messina, then plunged deep into the interior. By the end of that year they controlled most of the east coast and were making inroads towards Palermo.

In the second year, however, the advance abruptly halted. Besieging fortresses took time and Robert was impatient to bring the Muslims to battle. The stress of a long campaign was also beginning to show as the brothers started arguing about the division of spoils. Neither could completely agree about who was actually in charge, so they settled on an awkward joint rule. This was a particularly bad idea as Robert had no patience for consolidation and was easily bored. His attention in any case was needed on the mainland; long absences invited revolts and his restless barons hardly needed the encouragement. For the next ten years he put in sporadic appearances, leaving the conquest of Sicily largely in Roger's capable hands.

In the meantime Robert continued to put pressure on the southern Italian city of Bari and in the spring of 1071 it finally fell, extinguishing the last vestiges of the Roman Empire in Italy[4]. Guiscard entered the city in triumph, dressed in the Greek style and surrounded by his closest supporters. He was the sole master of southern Italy and had at last made his dukedom a reality. For another man this might have been enough. His enemies at home were cowed and peaceful, the pope had turned from being a rival into an ally, and there was no one left to challenge his authority throughout the south. But Guiscard was already dreaming of greater things. Something in the pageantry of Bari had caught his imagination. He had seen it in the palaces and churches of Sicily and in the luxury of captured imperial baggage. The landless knight who had made himself a duke turned his eyes thoughtfully to the East. There, glittering Byzantium, the biggest prize of all, was waiting.

Chapter Ten

THE IMPERIAL CROWN

A t sixty-five years old (elderly by medieval standards), Robert Guiscard deserved a rest. Most men his age were settling down to enjoy the fruits of their labour, which in Robert's case were plentiful. There were always the pleasures of hunting in the Apulian countryside or relaxing in one of his many palaces to distract him. But Guiscard had no intention of retiring. He was far too easily bored; he infinitely preferred fighting to governing and in any case he had become obsessed with the Byzantine Empire.

The past two decades of fighting Byzantium had left their mark. He had started by copying parts of the imperial seals into his own, and had then graduated to using the Byzantine title 'dux imperator' in his public decrees. This was equal parts vanity and shrewdness. Most of his subjects were thoroughly hellenized and posing as a Byzantine successor added a bit of legitimacy to his rule. Just in case anyone missed the point, he had a copy made of the imperial robes of state that he was careful to don at every opportunity.

All this strutting gained the attention of Constantinople, which was under disastrous attack by the Turks and wanted to make peace with the Normans as quickly as possible. Emperor Michael VII had a young son named Constantine, and Guiscard had a young daughter named Helena; a marriage proposal was arranged and the Norman duke was promised a fancy new title. He could now call himself nobelissimus (only a step below a Caesar) could wear the color purple, and could, reasonably hope that one day a descendant of his would sit on the imperial throne. Young Helena was shipped off to Constantinople, and Guiscard sat back to congratulate himself on a nice bit of diplomacy.

Unfortunately for him, events in Constantinople moved faster still. Just after Helena arrived, the emperor was overthrown by an old general named Nicephorus III. The Norman princess was dispatched to a convent and her prospective husband, Constantine, was exiled. The news of it all was disappointing for Guiscard, but only momentarily. The Byzantines were weak, overextended against the Turks, and vulnerable. An attack now would almost certainly yield great fruit. In the meantime, Helena was a convenient pawn with which to provoke a war.

The first step was to make an ultimatum that would be rejected out of hand. Playing the part of aggrieved father, Guiscard demanded that his daughter be instantly restored to favor, married to Constantine, and crowned empress. This would have been political suicide for Nicephorus. He could hardly start honoring the son of the man he had displaced, so he sensibly refused. Guiscard immediately declared war and started marshalling a great invading army. To bolster his effort, he found a wandering monk whom he claimed was the deposed emperor Michael – somehow escaped from captivity just in time to give an official blessing to the invasion. The ruse didn't fool anyone since the monk wasn't a particularly good actor, but Guiscard hardly cared. He had gotten his war and now he was going to claim his throne.

It took nearly a year to raise an army, but the effort produced

a magnificent result. Medieval western armies didn't tend
to be particularly diverse, but Robert had recruited soldiers
from all over southern Italy: Muslims from Sicily mixed with
Lombards and Greeks from Apulia and Calabria, while French
and Norman adventurers filled out the rest. Cities all along the
Italian coast were conscripted to build ships, and when they
couldn't fill the demand, additional ones were bought from
the heavily forested Croatian coast. By the spring of 1081 there
were one hundred and fifty ships waiting to transport twenty
thousand soldiers, horses and besieging equipment across the
Aegean. All that was needed was the command from the sixty-
four-year-old Guiscard. However, before he could give it, the
ground in Constantinople shifted again. Nicephorus III was
overthrown by a brilliant young general named Alexius, who
sent word that he was prepared to recognize all of Guiscard's
demands. The disgraced Constantine was to be restored as co-
emperor, Helena was to be rescued from her convent, and the
pair would be married.

Guiscard's temper was legendary, and his rage on this
occasion was especially fierce. The poor emissary who brought
the news expecting that it would be gladly received had to
flee from the chamber in fear for his life, and for two days the
Norman duke sulked in his tent in a black mood refusing to see
visitors. Alexius had neatly cut the ground out from under his
feet, but the preparations had come too far to stop. Guiscard's
eldest son, Bohemond, was sent with an advance guard to
form a bridgehead, and a month later Guiscard followed with
the main army.

By June the Normans had reached Durrës[1], the second
largest imperial city, nestled at the head of the old Roman road
that led to Constantinople. It was well defended and seemingly
impregnable, situated on a high peninsula and guarded by

marshes on the landward side. Guiscard attempted to talk it into submission and nearly succeeded, but the defenders were confident they could hold out and that the emperor wouldn't abandon them to their fate. A few days later, they were given dramatic evidence of the imperial attention. The Venetian fleet, bribed by Alexius, showed up without warning and engaged the Norman ships in battle. Using submerged pipes, they funneled Greek Fire[2] underneath the Norman vessels, burning them below the waterline.

Guiscard was now in a difficult position. Without naval support an effective blockade was impossible and there seemed to be little hope of taking the city by storm. Even worse, winter was approaching with the familiar problems of shelter, fuel, and maintaining supply lines in a hostile country. Morale plummeted, and an outbreak of dysentery swept through the ranks, further demoralizing everyone. Soldiers began to talk openly about retreat, but Guiscard wasn't the type of man to back down, so he burned his remaining ships to prevent desertions. For the common knight it must have seemed as if they were trapped in a nightmare. The defenders of Durrës sensed the mood and began an ominous new chant. The emperor Alexius was on his way, they said, at the head of a massive relief army.

Alexius Comnenus was a formidable opponent. Claiming descent from one of the patrician families of ancient Rome, he was a rare combination of military and political brilliance. At the age of forty he had never lost a battle and was the empire's most acclaimed general. Byzantium was in desperate need of such a man. Marauding Turks were overrunning the eastern frontiers, Slavs and Bulgars were invading from the west, and incompetent leadership in Constantinople only accelerated the pace of disintegration. By the decade's end there had been frantic appeals to the one general capable of stopping the bleeding, and Alexius obliged, easily expelling the elderly occupant of the palace.

Despite the new emperor's unblemished military record, however, the Norman invasion presented a serious problem. The chaos afflicting the empire had reduced the army to a disorganized mess and it would have to be rebuilt from the ground up. There was still a highly effective core – the famous Varangian Guard – but the rest was a mix of undisciplined militias, mercenaries, and private bodyguards. It wasn't exactly an inspiring force, but for the moment it would have to do. The empire was under attack and there was no time for training or drills.

Both Alexius and Guiscard had reasons to avoid the battle. While the Norman lines were weakened with disease, they were still frighteningly potent, and the emperor would have liked to let the coming winter soften them up a bit more. He also doubted the loyalty of his mercenaries and had good reason to suspect that they would desert at the first sign of trouble. Robert, on the other hand, was now caught between the imperial army and a heavily fortified city, and was unenthusiastic about initiating a battle. His normal practice would have been to withdraw to find a more suitable position to attack, but thanks to his rash decision to scuttle the fleet that was no longer an option.

The only ones actually looking forward to the fight were the Varangians. Fifteen years earlier, William the Conqueror had burst into England, killing the rightful king and subjecting the Anglo-Saxons to an increasingly brutal reign. Many of those who found life intolerable under the Norman boot eventually made their way to Constantinople where they enlisted in the ranks of the Guard. Now at last they were face to face with the hated foreigners who had despoiled their homes, murdered their families, and stolen their possessions. Hastings could finally be avenged.

Guiscard led the first attack against the center of the Byzantine line. The Normans had never yet encountered an enemy that could stand up to a cavalry charge, but against the wall of Varangians, it was the Normans who broke. Repeated charges were no more effective, and the Varangians began to slowly advance, wading into the Norman line with their wicked, double-headed axes. Unfortunately for Alexius, the rest of the Byzantine army failed to follow their lead. His Turkish auxiliaries chose this moment to desert, and the hopelessly outnumbered Varangians were left exposed and surrounded. The few that managed to escape fled to a nearby chapel dedicated to the archangel Michael, but there was no sanctuary against the Norman fury. The church and all within were burned to the ground.

The defeat seemed to sap the remaining strength from Byzantine territory. Durrës surrendered after another week of symbolic resistance and the rest of northern Greece wasn't far behind. When Guiscard reached Macedonia, the town of Kastoria surrendered without a fight, despite being guarded by three hundred Varangians. If even the elite forces of the empire were not loyal, then Constantinople was as good as won, and Guiscard boasted that he would be in the capital in time for Christmas. For once, however, he had met his match. Alexius couldn't stop the Normans with a sword, but he still had his pen, and where armies had failed, diplomacy would succeed.

Southern Italy was a tinderbox waiting to explode, filled with barons and nobles who resented the Norman yoke and who despised their subservient status. They were held in check only by fear, each of them unwilling to take the first step.

Alexius merely had to provide some motivation. Byzantine agents were sent to Italy loaded down with bags of gold whispering that now was the time to strike. Almost overnight the peninsula flared into open revolt. The man Guiscard had left to represent him southern Italy wrote desperately to his master that if he didn't return soon he wouldn't have a home to return to.

Guiscard hesitated as long as he could. The longer he let the rebellion fester, the more difficult it would be to suppress. But he had Byzantium on its heels and the invasion was sure to falter in his absence. Valuable ground would be lost and the wily Alexius would have time to recover. Finally, in the early months of 1082 news arrived that forced his hand. The German emperor, Henry IV, was marching on Rome and the frantic pope was calling for Norman protection at once. Taking a public oath to remain unshaven and unwashed until he returned, Guiscard left the army in his son Bohemond's care and left for Italy.

Pope Gregory VII was a strange ally for the rough Norman duke. Idealistic, principled, and inflexible, he was the last person who would be expected to stand by the morally ambivalent Guiscard. Necessity, however, had driven them together. Gregory was involved in a great controversy, which had thrown Christendom into turmoil. He was attempting to break the Church free from secular control and had clashed with the German emperor, Henry IV. The first victory had belonged to the pope. Henry had been excommunicated and forced to trek barefoot in the middle of winter to the remote castle of Canossa in northern Italy, and beg Gregory to lift the sentence. That had merely been the opening salvo, however, and as soon as he was strong enough the emperor had threatened to bring his army to Rome and appoint a new pope if Gregory wouldn't back down. Gregory needed a defender, and there was only one figure in Italy capable of being one. Swallowing his pride, he had offered Guiscard legitimacy and papal support in exchange for protection. The deal worked well enough until Guiscard left to invade Byzantium. A letter from Alexius, along with a few bags of gold, had found their way to emperor Henry urging him to descend on defenseless Italy. The emperor, of course, hardly needed to be asked twice.

Henry's army had little problem breaking into Rome. Gregory fled to Hadrian's mausoleum[3] and just managed to hold out. His supporters still controlled the left bank of the Tiber, and disease began to decimate the imperial ranks. Henry withdrew with most of his forces to higher ground and settled in for a siege.

Guiscard meanwhile was busy trying to stamp out the revolt in southern Italy, ignoring the pope's increasingly panicked letters. By the end of 1084 he had crushed the last resistance and could have come to Gregory's aid but he hesitated. As he had feared, the Byzantine campaign was in serious trouble, and if he didn't return immediately there was the real possibility of a complete collapse. On the other hand, his attention was simultaneously needed in Rome, where a valuable ally was fighting for his life. For one of the only times in his life, Robert Guiscard didn't know what to do.

Once again, however, the decision was made for him by outside forces, this time by the Romans themselves. They were tired of Gregory, blaming his inflexibility for the long siege and severe privation, and they opened the gates and invited Henry to take full possession of Rome. The emperor entered in triumph, declared Gregory deposed, and appointed his own candidate. Guiscard now had no choice but to act. If Gregory was destroyed then so was the Hauteville legitimacy.

Byzantium would have to wait. Gathering a massive army from every part of his domain, he marched on Rome.

Henry was not foolish enough to be there when Guiscard arrived. His weakened army was no match for the Normans and he knew it. Three days before Guiscard appeared, the emperor advised the Romans to defend themselves as best they could and then slipped away. The panicked inhabitants of the city barred the gates, but they were doomed. The walls of the city had been built 800 years before during the reign of the emperor Aurelian and hadn't been significantly updated since. Within minutes of Guiscard's first attack, his soldiers broke in and fanned out through the city, killing and looting as they went. Gregory was escorted from Hadrian's mausoleum to the Lateran in triumph and once again seated on the papal throne.

The victory, however, was a pyrrhic one. The Muslim and Greek contingents of Guiscard's army saw the city as their prize to plunder and started a frenzy of rape and murder. After three days of this treatment the cowed citizens were pushed to their limit and took to the streets, waging a desperate guerrilla campaign against the invaders. Any semblance of order vanished in the chaos and the Normans, realizing they had lost control, started setting fires in an attempt to flush out their enemies. The damage was immense. What wasn't burned down was despoiled. From the Lateran to the Coliseum, barely a building was left standing. Neither churches, nor palaces, nor ancient pagan temples were spared.

Gregory had been restored, but he was now so universally hated that he had to accompany Guiscard's army when it withdrew. He found a new home in Salerno, where he set up his court in exile, and concentrated on his reform of the Church. He died the following year and was buried, as was fitting, in a Norman tomb. He was defiant until the end, but his last words were bitter: "I have loved righteousness and hated iniquity, therefore I die in exile".

Robert Guiscard, meanwhile, was finally free to concentrate on Byzantium. The war had not gone well without him. His son, Bohemond, was a superb knight and a good general, but he lacked his father's ability to inspire. Despite demolishing three successive armies that the emperor had sent against him, the mood in the Norman camp was increasingly defeatist. It had been nearly four years since they had sailed from Italy, and yet they were no closer to taking Constantinople than on the day they had arrived. Most of them were exhausted and homesick, beginning to feel as if this long campaign would never end. Bohemond managed to hold them together for a few more months, but at the end of the campaigning season he committed the cardinal sin of underestimating his opponent. As he was crossing a river in northern Greece, Alexius lured him into attacking a decoy force while the main imperial army plundered the Norman baggage. After an afternoon spent chasing shadows, Bohemond returned to his camp to find that four years' worth of spoils had vanished. For the weary army it was the last straw. The moment Bohemond's back was turned the men surrendered en masse to Alexius.

It was a severe setback, but Guiscard was nothing if not persistent. Although he was now seventy, he had lost none of his vigor and he immediately gathered another army. He spent the winter in Corfu, but typhoid fever struck the camp, killing thousands. When it finally abated, he gave orders to sail to the Byzantine island of Cephalonia as the first step of the campaign. In the middle of the crossing, however, Guiscard himself was struck by the fever and was barely strong enough to stand when he arrived. He died on July 17, 1085, having never lost a major battle.

The body was taken back to Italy, but just off the coast of Otranto the corpse washed overboard in a storm and was badly damaged. The sailors managed to recover it, but the decision was made to remove the heart and entrails and bury them in a small chapel while the rest was embalmed and completed the journey to the Hauteville mausoleum in Venosa, Italy. There it was interred in the Abbey of the Holy Trinity in a magnificent tomb.

He had lived an extraordinary life, and his accomplishments had earned him a spot as one of the greatest military adventurers in history. With a mixture of vision, political skill, and force of personality he had taken a small barony and turned it into one of the great powers of Europe. Along the way he had evicted the Byzantines from Italy, the Muslims from Sicily, saved the reformed papacy, and held two emperors at bay. An anonymous stone worker put it best in an inscription above his tomb: "Here lies Guiscard, Terror of the World..."

Chapter Eleven

BOHEMOND I

Guiscard's death left the vexing question of who would inherit his possessions unanswered. The trouble was that although his two marriages had produced at least ten children, his most able son wasn't a legitimate one.

The boy had been born sometime before 1058 and was given the Christian name of 'Marc'. A few nights before the birth, Guiscard had been regaled at a banquet with the story of a legendary giant named Buamundas Gigas, and when he saw the large size of the baby he nicknamed him 'Bohemond,' unwittingly inventing one of the more popular names of the Middle Ages.

Almost nothing is known of Bohemond's early years, although he evidently had some schooling since he could read and write Latin along with a smattering of Greek and possibly Arabic. When he was still young, perhaps only four, Guiscard abandoned his mother for political reasons. Although Bohemond was now both illegitimate and disinherited, there didn't seem to be too many hard feelings as he was raised by his step-mother and given an important post in Guiscard's army as soon as he was old enough. Perhaps this was because, regardless of the temporary needs of realpolitik, there was no doubting who his father was. Bohemond looked every inch a Hauteville. With the broad shoulders, thick chest, and blond hair of his Viking ancestors, he was enormously tall, with an easy air of command. Even the restless and reckless streaks of his father were there. As one of his contemporaries put it, "He is always seeking the impossible".

Bohemond got his chance for adventure in 1081 when Guiscard decided to invade the Byzantine Empire. The twenty-seven-year-old was sent with an advance guard and instructed to lay waste to the Dalmatian[1] countryside, capture the port city of Valona to use as a bridgehead, and besiege the island of Corfu. The only serious resistance he faced was at Corfu, where the defenders openly mocked his small force, but when they saw Guiscard's main fleet on the horizon, the garrison fled in terror.

From there, however, the campaign had unraveled. Guiscard's plan – so we are told – was to put Bohemond on the throne of Constantinople, and carve out a larger empire of his own to the east, but he was outwitted by the Byzantine emperor Alexius. When the emperor's gold had forced Guiscard to return, Bohemond had been ordered to secure Greece and Macedonia, and warned not to risk a battle with the emperor. Bohemond's failure in the subsequent campaign had not been due to any lack of courage on his part. The emperor was simply too experienced and wily.

When Bohemond entered northern Greece and began to systematically reduce some Byzantine fortresses, Alexius suddenly appeared. As the two armies prepared themselves for a battle, the emperor sent light chariots bristling with spears into the Norman line. It would have crippled the main section of the army, but Bohemond had been warned and was expecting the ruse. As the chariots approached, gaps in the line opened up and they passed harmlessly through. The Normans then charged the Byzantines and easily routed the half-trained recruits.

Alexius regrouped in the Balkan city of Ohrid[2], and a few months later he tried again. This time he had his men scatter nails across the center of the field the night before the battle, hoping to cripple the Norman cavalry as they charged. Again Bohemond was warned, and in the morning he held his center back and ordered his wings to collapse on the Byzantine army. They broke almost immediately and this time Bohemond pursued Alexius into the Balkan Mountains, capturing Ohrid, the emperor's previous city of refuge.

Although Bohemond had been successful at every turn, that winter was a demoralizing one. There was little food and less money to be had, and the Norman troops hadn't been paid for several months. Some began to question exactly what they were doing in a strange and inhospitable land. Constantinople, which had seemed so close a year ago, now seemed increasingly distant. That spring, Alexius attacked for the third time. The Normans were occupying the ancient Greek city of Larissa – birthplace of Achilles – when the imperial standards appeared and began to advance. Bohemond immediately charged, chasing the fleeing Byzantines for several miles. Alexius, however, wasn't with them; he was leading the main army into the Norman camp, capturing two years' worth of spoils.

Thinking he had won another victory, Bohemond was relaxing by a river, eating grapes and lampooning yet another example of Byzantine cowardice when the message reached him that his camp was under attack. He raced back with his cavalry, but was too late. He managed to repulse an overeager Byzantine charge, but was forced to retreat and collect his scattered men, abandoning all the territory he had conquered that year to Alexius.

The emperor sensed that the tide was turning in his favor, and he opened up secret negotiations with Bohemond's officers.

He cleverly suggested that they demand their full pay, knowing that with the recent loss of supplies, Bohemond had no way of paying it. He further offered lucrative posts in the imperial army (which he backed up with substantial gifts), or safe passage home if their honor prevented them from accepting.

Some of Bohemond's officers undoubtedly stayed loyal, but enough of them demanded their pay that he was forced to return to Italy to raise the money. The moment he was gone, whatever morale remained collapsed and with one exception, his officers defected to Alexius. Bohemond received word of their treachery as he was boarding his ship in the Dalmatian seaport. The war was lost. Not by any glorious defeat, but by a thousand cuts. Perhaps not wanting to face his father until tempers had a time to cool, Bohemond wintered on the Dalmatian coast, waiting until the spring to return to Italy.

Fortunately for Bohemond, Guiscard was not particularly upset. He had had his own hands full putting down the Italian revolt, but he had settled it in such a ruthless fashion that it would take more gold than Alexius had to stir up trouble again. Now the emperor would have his undivided attention. That October of 1084 Guiscard and his four adult sons sailed again. They were intercepted by the Venetian navy, which scattered them, but when the fastest ships left prematurely to inform Venice of the great victory, the Normans rallied and managed to defeat them.

It was too late in the season for much more campaigning, so the Normans wintered on Corfu. While they were confined, Bohemond came down with a fever and obtained permission from his father to return to Italy to convalesce. In his absence Guiscard caught the fever as well, and after lingering a few months he died.

Bohemond was the natural choice to succeed him. Not

only was he battle-seasoned, commanding and ambitious, but the only serious rival – his half-brother Roger Borsa[3] – was just thirteen years old, and was already displaying the nervous incompetence that would be the hallmark of his later years. But fatefully, Roger Borsa – or more correctly, his mother – was present at Guiscard's deathbed while Bohemond was away in Italy. She convinced the assembled Normans that her son – a legitimate heir – was the only choice to inherit Guiscard's lands and titles. Surprisingly, she found a powerful ally for this argument in Bohemond's uncle, Roger of Sicily. Whoever was chosen would technically be his senior colleague, and he naturally wanted someone he could manipulate. Bohemond, still recovering in Italy, was dispossessed of his inheritance for a second time.

Roger Borsa and his mother had pulled off a clever coup, but if they thought the matter was settled, they didn't know Bohemond very well. He was furious, and as soon as his uncle was safely back in Sicily, he started a rebellion. Roger Borsa tried to buy off his half-brother with the best part of southern Apulia, but that only encouraged Bohemond to try for more land. Bohemond crossed the border into Calabria and convinced the most powerful of his brother's vassals there to switch loyalty. The revolt gradually spread throughout Calabria until Roger Borsa desperately called for his uncle's help. The elder Roger responded to maintain the status quo, and forced Bohemond to agree to a truce, essentially allowing him to keep what he had conquered. This uneasy peace lasted for three years until Roger Borsa fell seriously ill with a fever. Assuming that his half-brother was dead, Bohemond moved quickly to seize his property, claiming to be acting to 'protect the interests of his nephews'.

Once again, their uncle Roger had to cross over from

Sicily and restrain Bohemond from capturing any more of his half-brother's lands. This basic pattern continued for the next several years, with Bohemond attempting to chip away at Borsa's territory without being serious enough to draw in his uncle too frequently. The slow-burning civil war that resulted mostly benefited Roger of Sicily. Each time he intervened, he obtained more concessions from his weak nephew. Family relations all around were understandably strained.

In the summer of 1096, the city of Amalfi rebelled against Borsa and a frustrated Bohemond was summoned by their uncle Roger to join them as a sign of family solidarity against the rebels. After nine years of a fruitless civil war, it was clear to a depressed Bohemond that his uncle would never allow him to have any significant power. Just as he was resigning himself to this fate, however, a new opportunity presented itself. The year before, Pope Urban II had put out a great call for a 'crusade' to free the Holy Land, and eager knights had begun to trickle into southern Italy in search of a sea passage. At first they had been mostly Italian, and Bohemond had ignored them as a fad, but as he sat before the walls of Amalfi larger groups of French knights began to appear, and he realized the international scope of the movement.

He would never be more than an upstart in Italy, forever held down by his uncle, but now his father's old dream beckoned to the East. If he couldn't claim a title here in the West he could carve out a kingdom for himself in the Levant, and the crusade would provide the perfect cover. All that was left was for him to announce his intentions, which he did with considerable panache. In the middle of the siege he called a great assembly where he dramatically swore to liberate Jerusalem and called all good Christians to join him. He then took off his rich, scarlet cloak and ripped it up to make crosses for his vassals and those who were quickest to kneel. The bulk of those present eagerly joined in, providing him with an army suitable to his rank while depriving the two Rogers of theirs at the same time. His annoyed kinsman had no choice but to abandon the siege.

The Crusades are usually thought of as single armies, or single waves of armies, launching themselves in a certain year. However, they were more like continuous movements; not armies so much as armed men moving in ebbs and flows to the East. There was no single route they chose to travel, and no single recognized leader, just a vague agreement of the leading princes to gather at Constantinople.

The lack of an overall commander meant almost certain bickering and disorganization, but Bohemond correctly saw it also as a golden opportunity. Of all the princes, he was by far the most experienced and ambitious. If a general commander was needed, and it almost certainly would be, he was the natural candidate. Always with an eye to the future, he was careful to act the part of dignified statesman.

While the forces led by other princes behaved with reckless abandon, pillaging their way across Byzantine territory and frequently skirmishing with their imperial escorts, Bohemond was an example of order and decorum. Everything had been carefully prepared beforehand. Together with his nephew Tancred[4] and a small but very well-trained army, Bohemond set sail from the Italian town of Bari and landed his men at various points on the Dalmatian coast in order not to overwhelm local food supplies. He had taken the precaution of forbidding looting on pain of death so as to prevent the ill-will that usually accompanied a march through foreign territory.

The route he chose was a difficult one – twelve hundred meters above sea level through mountain passes in the early winter – but his planning was such that he made it without incident into western Macedonia by Christmas. From there he traveled along the Via Egnatia, the same road on which a decade before he had marched with his father in their failed bid to conquer Constantinople. This time, of course, he was on his best behavior, scrupulously maintaining cordial relations with the imperial guard which was sent to keep tabs on his progress.

At Epirus he sent a messenger to Constantinople, asking for an audience with emperor Alexius. He wasn't the first crusader to reach the imperial city, and he was anxious to see what the other western leaders had agreed to. Most of all, he wanted to make sure that none of his rivals had received special treatment from the emperor.

Westerner knights tended to assume that the Byzantines were soft and weak, but Bohemond knew better than any how powerful the empire still was. It was by far the most significant Christian state in the Near East, and without its support, no permanent success could be achieved. Friendship would also have other benefits. A special recognition from Alexius would put him in control of all crusader dealings with the empire; he would be the pivotal figure of the grand Christian alliance, and the de facto leader of the crusade.

The treatment he received when he reached Constantinople was encouraging. After a stay of only a single night[5] in the monastery of Saints Cosmas and Damian he was given a special escort to the imperial palace, an honor accorded to no other westerner. There he was showered with gifts and impressive-sounding (although empty) titles and admitted into the emperor's presence.

Once there, standing before the immense imperial throne complete with golden lions that would stand up and roar at the touch of a lever, he was asked to take an oath of fealty to

Alexius and to promise to return any land he conquered to the empire. He gave it without a moment's hesitation, and in return asked to be named Grand Domestic of the East – the commander-in-chief of all imperial forces in Asia.

Bohemond had played his part to perfection, but the emperor Alexius was too perceptive to be taken in by him. Outwardly he gave every sign of embracing Bohemond, but he didn't trust him an inch, and he had no intention of increasing his already dangerous power. He had hoped to pawn off Bohemond with expensive gifts, and was now slightly embarrassed that he had asked so boldly for a title. So he stalled, saying that the time wasn't right to name him Grand Domestic, while vaguely hinting that he could earn it with a show of energy and loyalty.

That was the best Bohemond could get, so with a few parting pleasantries and a promise by the emperor to send troops and food with him, Bohemond withdrew and rejoined his army. They were ferried across the Bosphorus and marched to Nicaea where the main Crusader army was already besieging the city. Thanks to his timely arrival and the much-needed supplies, Bohemond saw an immediate surge in his popularity. This was increased when he defeated a Turkish relieving army, triumphantly binding the Muslim captives with the very ropes they had brought to tie up the Crusaders.

Bohemond's run of good luck continued with the fall of Nicaea. Relations with Byzantium plummeted when the Turks decided to surrender to the Byzantine contingent who slipped into the city at night and refused to let the Crusaders enter to engage in the traditional three days of pillaging. Under the circumstances, his failure to get Alexius' endorsement was now if anything a badge of honor.

When the army decided to move on in the direction of

Antioch, Bohemond suggested that they split in half to make it easier to find supplies. He accompanied the advance group while his main competitor, Raymond of Toulouse, the only other crusader of comparable standing, took control of the second wing which was traveling a day behind. Near the town of Dorylaeum, Bohemond was ambushed, but thanks to his quick thinking, disaster was averted. A message was sent to Raymond to hurry, while the Turks, who mistakenly believed that they had trapped the entire army, repeatedly attacked. When Raymond appeared with a fresh group of knights the Turks fled, leaving the treasury and household goods of their emir behind.

The victory was credited to both commanders, and the entire army spent a welcome respite among the orchards and streams of the nearby old Byzantine city of Iconium. The Turks made one more attempt to stop them from crossing the Taurus Mountains, but this time Bohemond nearly defeated them by himself, charging straight at the emir and engaging him in single combat. Unnerved, the Turks fled, abandoning any further attempt to block the Crusaders' path. That night a comet flared in the sky, seeming to symbolize both the victory and Bohemond's stratospheric prestige.

The Norman, as always, sensing an opportunity, detached himself from the main army and went off to liberate several neighboring cities. These he discreetly turned over to the emperor as proof of his good faith, and a subtle reminder that he was still available for appointment as Grand Domestic of the East. In his absence, a rumor reached the Crusader camp that Antioch was unguarded, and Raymond of Toulouse, still smarting from Bohemond's string of victories, quickly dispatched five hundred men to occupy it in his name.

Unfortunately for Raymond, the rumor turned out to be

false, as Muslim reinforcements were pouring into Antioch. His men arrived to find it impregnable, an opinion which the rest of the army shared when they showed up several weeks later.

Antioch was one of the great cities of the East, and had only been captured from the Byzantines by Muslim forces twelve years before by treachery. The city spread three and a half square miles across the valley floor at the foot of Mount Silpius and was surrounded by walls built by emperor Justinian more than five hundred years earlier, complete with six major gates and studded with four hundred towers. Inside the circuit of those walls rose a spur of the mountain, at whose thousand-foot summit was a massive citadel. The mountainous terrain made approach from the south, east, or west difficult, while at the same time the sheer length of the walls made a siege virtually impossible. Bohemond had been looking for a suitable Eastern capital for himself, and the moment he saw Antioch's magnificent defenses he realized that he had found it. The stated goal of the crusade was to liberate Jerusalem, but if he could install himself here there would be no need to go a step further.

The Crusaders constructed three siege towers and attempted to starve the city into submission, but they simply lacked the numbers to cut it off completely. The Orontes river supplied it with fresh water, and foraging parties easily evaded crusader patrols. Even worse, the Crusaders soon exhausted the surrounding food supply, and were often ambushed by roving bands of defenders. With the winter came earthquakes and freezing snowstorms, while in the night sky the aurora borealis flashed, adding fear to the general gloom. Several desperate attempts to take the city failed miserably and news arrived that an enormous Muslim relief army under the command of the terrible Kerbogha of Mosul was on its way. By the spring, one in seven crusaders was dying of hunger, and mass defections began.

Bohemond had long since come to the conclusion that Antioch was impossible to take by assault, and if force wasn't an option, then duplicity was clearly the key. Somehow, he contacted a traitor inside the city who agreed to surrender one of the defensive towers to him. All that was left was for Bohemond to choose his moment.

First he had to get rid of any rival claims to the city. There was still a small Byzantine contingent with the army that was hoping to take control of Antioch once it was captured. Bohemond summoned its leader into his tent and hinted that there was a plan to murder him, which he of course had regrettably been unable to stamp out. Although false, this rumor was easy enough to believe, and the next day the man abruptly left with his retinue. Bohemond turned around and announced that the Byzantines had left out of cowardice, abandoning them all to their fate. The Crusaders had given an oath that they would return Antioch to the empire, but now that could safely be ignored.

Bohemond next announced that he was contemplating leaving because of pressing needs in Italy. His words had the appropriate effect. He had played a leading role in every military encounter and the thought of losing him now as Kerbogha was closing in terrified the army. The Crusading princes, of course, saw it for the bluster that it was, but they were powerless in the face of public opinion. When Bohemond then floated the idea that Antioch would be an acceptable compensation to any losses sustained at home, even Raymond of Toulouse had to bow to the inevitable.

After they had agreed to give him the city, he confided that he had a contact on the inside and told them his plan. The army would break camp and march out as if to confront the approaching Kerbogha. Under cover of darkness they would return and slip into the city through an unguarded postern gate that the traitor would leave unlocked.

Two hours before dawn, Bohemond led sixty soldiers up a ladder, and quickly took over two nearby towers and the walls between. With the help of the native Christians of the city, a city gate was flung open and the army poured inside. By nightfall there wasn't a Turk alive. More than seven months after they had first arrived, Antioch was finally in Crusader hands.

The ordeal wasn't quite over, however. Although the city had fallen, the citadel was still controlled by the Turks. Bohemond had been wounded in his lone attempt to take it, and (far more seriously) Kerbogha was on his way with an army seventy-five-thousand strong. The first problem was easy enough to deal with. Bohemond built a wall around the citadel to prevent an attack from it, then turned his mind to the defense of his new city. Two days later Kerbogha arrived.

The Crusaders were in a desperate situation. The seven-month siege had depleted the city's food supplies and there had been no time to restock them. The situation was so dire that some knights resorted to slaughtering their own horses for food. To make matters worse, deserters had informed Kerbogha of the situation. He attempted a ferocious assault against the section of walls that Bohemond was defending and was only beaten back with the greatest difficulty. Well aware that the Crusaders were on the verge of collapse, he settled back into a siege.

Only a miracle could save the trapped Christians now, but fortunately for them, a miracle arrived. A French hermit named Peter Bartholomew claimed that a saint had appeared and revealed to him the site of the Holy Lance – the spear that the centurion had used to pierce Christ's side. Assisted by the hosts of heaven and led by this powerful relic they could put Kerbogha to flight.

It's not likely that Bohemond was convinced by this tale, after all he had probably seen the original lance in Constantinople, but he knew the effect it would have on morale, and when Peter dramatically dug beneath the floor of the city's cathedral and found a rusted piece of metal, he was among the first to declare that it was real. He ordered five days of fasting, and leaving only two hundred men in the city, he marched out behind the lance for an all-out attack.

The sight of the Crusader army, with many of its starving knights stumbling along on foot, was probably more pathetic than terrifying, but despite that, Bohemond's charge was well timed. Kerbogha's own alliance was crumbling. Most of his emirs mistrusted him, and feared that success at Antioch would make him too powerful. So when the Crusaders emerged from the city, they chose to desert. Kerbogha's remaining forces still outnumbered the Crusaders, but they were unnerved by the size of the Crusader force and set fire to the grass between the armies to delay them. The wind blew the smoke in the Turkish faces, and what had started as a tactical withdrawal turned into a rout. Armenian and Syrian herdsmen, meanwhile, seeing the chance for revenge for a decade of oppression, came down from the hills to join the slaughter.

The victory was complete. The Turkish defenders of the citadel had watched the debacle unfold in front of them and knew that all hope was now lost. Much to Bohemond's gratification they announced that they would only surrender to him personally, sending one last snub to his old rival Raymond of Toulouse who was ill and had been forced to observe the entire thing from the sidelines.

Raymond didn't take the news well. He dug in his heels,

refusing to acknowledge Bohemond as master of Antioch. His obstinacy brought the entire crusade to a screeching halt, but there were more than just petty reasons for his stance. Like Bohemond, he wanted to be recognized as the supreme commander of the crusade, and he was shrewd enough to realize that despite any personal distaste for the Byzantines, they were needed if the crusade had any hope of long-term success. Turning over Antioch, one of the empire's main cities, to Bohemond would permanently sever relations with Constantinople.

The Crusader leaders were evenly split between Bohemond and Raymond, and they dithered for several months. During this time a typhoid epidemic hit and morale – euphoric after the victory – once again sank. The rank and file didn't really care which of their leaders got control of Antioch, in fact they hardly cared about Antioch at all. They had signed on to liberate Jerusalem, and the longer they stayed squabbling in Asia Minor, the angrier they became.

Finally, with the army reaching the point of mutiny, Raymond and Bohemond came to a compromise. Bohemond would get Antioch and in return he would recognize Raymond as the leader of the crusade. After fifteen months in Antioch the Crusading army finally marched off, leaving a well-pleased Bohemond behind.

It was his greatest moment of triumph. His aim in joining the crusade had never been to see Jerusalem, it had been to found his own state, and now he had one of the major cities of the Near East under his control. He was in a position to dominate both the lucrative pilgrim trade to Jerusalem and the nearby Crusader kingdoms that were being established. When he visited the newly-captured Jerusalem a few months later as Prince of Antioch, he was received as the most important regional power, easily securing the election of his own candidate as patriarch.

Unfortunately for Bohemond, his triumph was short lived. The very boldness which had won him his wealth and power, proved to be his undoing. In the summer of 1100 he left his nephew Tancred as regent of Antioch and marched north with only three hundred men to campaign on the upper Euphrates. Blundering into an ambush, he was captured and thrown into a Turkish prison. The emperor Alexius offered to pay his ransom if he was delivered to Constantinople, but Bohemond declined, and was forced to spend three years as a captive until Tancred could raise the funds to free him.

In his absence, Tancred had greatly increased the size of the principality, and as soon as he was free, Bohemond marched south to extend it further, only to be severely defeated again. Antioch was now caught between the twin rocks of Saracen and Byzantine power, and its army was too depleted to hold, much less expand in either direction. Only a massive infusion from Europe could salvage the situation, so in 1105, Bohemond left to drum up support for a new crusade.

The effort was a dramatic success. In Italy, crowds arrived to greet him wherever he stayed and in France, King Philip offered his daughter in marriage. He was widely seen as the hero of the First Crusade, and his popularity was such that the English king, Henry I, refused to let him land in England for fear that he would enlist too many nobles to his cause. Dazzled by his celebrity status, and finding an easy scapegoat for every misfortune in the Byzantines[6], Bohemond unwisely decided to revive his old dream of taking Constantinople's throne.

With a thirty-five-thousand-strong army he invaded the Dalmatian coast and attacked Durrës, the westernmost city of the empire. Unlike his previous two attempts, however, this time the Byzantines were in a position of strength.

While Alexius leisurely marched to confront the Normans, he persuaded the Venetian navy to attack Bohemond's fleet, which it easily destroyed. He then studiously avoided a direct confrontation while plague and the depredations of a siege depleted Bohemond's strength. With his escape route cut off and a series of disastrous skirmishes sapping morale, Bohemond was forced to conclude a humiliating truce.

It amounted to an unconditional surrender. Although he was allowed to keep Antioch, it was only as Alexius' vassal; all captured Byzantine territory had to be returned, and a Greek patriarch of Alexius' choosing had to be installed in the city's cathedral.

After a lifetime of struggle that had recently seen such dizzying triumphs, this last setback was too much. Bohemond refused to even return to Antioch, setting sail for Sicily instead, where he died a broken man three years later. His body was taken to the Italian city of Canosa and interred in a simple mausoleum, where it can still be seen today with the single word BOAMUNDUS marking the spot.

It was a pitiful end to a remarkable life. Thanks mostly to his nephew Tancred, the principality of Antioch endured, but it would never be the dominant power that Bohemond had envisioned. The energy and daring of the Normans, as well as their great legacy, was further west. Even as Bohemond expired, it was blooming in the sun-drenched island of Sicily.

Chapter Twelve

DEXTERA DOMINI

When Guiscard died, the Norman conquest of Sicily had been left unfinished. His lands in southern Italy convulsed in the usual power struggle between his sons, and it seemed for a moment as if the remarkable Norman advance had at last ended. No obvious leader of Robert's caliber rose to take his title, and the Sicilian campaign – the most important of the southern Norman fronts – devolved onto the shoulders of Guiscard's youngest brother.

Roger de Hauteville was an unlikely conqueror. The twelfth son of old Tancred, he was sixteen years younger than his famous sibling. He had always been a bit different from his brothers, less physically imposing but more thoughtful, displaying a rare talent among the Hautevilles for keeping his temper in check.

Not much is known about his early life other than the fact that he spent it on the family estate in Normandy. He probably had the same education as his siblings, spending his formative years apprenticed to a wealthier knight. By the time he was twenty-four, all but one of his brothers had left to seek their fortunes in the south. Roger might have been content to stay in the now-empty family home had it not been for a chance meeting with the beautiful Judith d'Evreux. Despite a huge gulf in social status – she was related to William the Conqueror – they fell in love, and before long Roger announced his intention to marry her. Unfortunately he had neither land nor wealth, and Judith's father wasn't amused by the thought of some lowly knight stealing his daughter away. If Roger wanted her hand he would have to find a suitable dowry, so he left for Italy to find fame and fortune.

It so happened that Roger's brother Guiscard was busy trying to subdue Calabria and was glad to make use of his skills. The two made daring raids along the coast and within five years had subdued the region. The experience seems to have given Roger a taste for more and he suggested a richer target. Just across the narrow straits of Messina, less than two miles from the Italian seacoast, was the Arab-controlled island of Sicily, now fortuitously in complete disarray.

The Arabs had first arrived in Sicily in the mid-ninth century from North Africa and spent the next hundred years wresting the island away from the Byzantines. They had finally conquered the last imperial outpost in 965 and settled down to enjoy the fruits of their labour. For a century Sicily was a relatively peaceful part of the North African Muslim Empire controlled by the city of Mahdia on the present-day Tunisian coast. But Mahdia was involved in the power struggles of the Islamic world; war with Cairo abroad and civil wars at home weakened its control over the island. As communications broke down, ethnic tensions in Sicily rose. The first Arab arrivals were resentful of the Berbers who crossed over from Mahdia in increasing numbers, and both groups distrusted the native Greeks. By the time Roger arrived in Italy, Sicily was split between three rival emirs, and a racial war had broken out between Arab and Berber. It was the perfect time to invade, and surprisingly enough, it was one of the emirs who offered the invitation.

Ibn Timnah was a rogue even by the standards of the time. He had seized control of Syracuse by killing his predecessor and helped himself to the man's widow. He then tried to expand into his neighbor's territory – that of the Emir of Messina who also happened to be his new wife's brother – with disastrous results. The humiliating treaty he had to sign was bad enough, but he made it worse by getting drunk and taking out his frustrations on his wife. She fled to her brother in Messina and in a rage he swore that he would have Ibn Timnah's head. The now quite sober emir was chased out of Syracuse and had to flee to Italy for safety. Finding Roger in Calabria he offered to partner with the Normans in exchange for a joint control of Sicily.

Roger couldn't have asked for a better invitation. Although it was the middle of winter and hardly the time to start a campaign, he gathered a force of a hundred and fifty knights and crossed the straits. At first all went well. The governor of Messina was tricked into an ambush and killed, and when the garrison rushed out to avenge him they were badly mauled by the Normans. Unfortunately, it was Roger's youthful enthusiasm that let them down. Seeing the chance to grab Messina and his own claim to greatness, he led a hasty attempt to rush the walls but was driven back with heavy losses. He retreated to the ships, but when he arrived at the beach he found that a storm had driven his fleet away. For three days the Normans were obliged to camp miserably on the beach fending, off the incessant Muslim attacks and trying to stay warm. Finally on the fourth day the Norman ships returned and Roger made his escape.

The campaign had been discouraging, but Roger remained determined. A few months later he tried again, this time with the help of his brother Guiscard, and the two of them mustered an army of nearly five hundred knights. The Muslims were alerted to the danger and kept up a watchful patrol of the channel, so the brothers came up with a ruse. While Guiscard positioned himself at the north end of the straits noisily preparing to cross, Roger slipped across at the southern end with half of the knights. He landed five miles from Messina and found the coast completely deserted. Marching towards the city he intercepted a Muslim baggage train carrying the entire payroll for the Messina garrison. This stroke of luck was followed by an even bigger one. The majority of Messina's defenders had marched north to repel Guiscard's expected crossing, leaving the walls bare. The moment his first soldier cleared the battlements the inhabitants surrendered and Roger's flag was hoisted above the city. The Muslim army on the coast, seeing the banner and realizing what had happened, fled into the interior.

The Normans now had a foothold in Sicily, but there was no time to sit back and enjoy it. After attending a thanksgiving service hosted by the city's Greek population, the brothers joined their Arab ally Ibn Timnah and headed deep into the island's central plateau. Their goal was to take the great fortress of Enna and deal a knockout blow to Ibn Timnah's brother-in-law, but when they arrived they found the castle impregnable. Even worse, the emir had gathered his entire army and was delighted that the pesky Normans had strayed so deeply into his territory. Seeing the chance to destroy them once and for all, he launched a ferocious assault.

It was the first time the Muslims of Sicily had come face to face with a Norman army, and it would be an experience that would be repeated many times with the same result over the next three decades. Although they far outnumbered the Normans, the light Arab cavalry stood no chance against the heavily armored knights. The battle was quick, and from the Muslim point of view, disastrous; thousands were killed or captured, and the survivors fled to the safety of their fortress and refused to come out again.

Enough spoils were taken from the battle to make every soldier who participated a wealthy man. The bewildered Arabs concluded that the Normans were invincible, and more importantly, the Normans believed it as well. In the coming years they would always be vastly outnumbered but would never hesitate to fight.

The brothers had won a stunning success, but were divided on how best to exploit it. Guiscard, as always, had concerns on the mainland where yet another revolt was beginning and needed to withdraw, but Roger wanted to continue the advance. There was no question of trying to storm Enna since they had no heavy siege equipment, but they could at least extract protection money from the surrounding towns and further erode the emir's support. As elder brother, Guiscard's argument eventually prevailed, but Roger stayed long enough to seize the town of Troina, a largely Greek settlement on a hill that enjoyed a strategic view of the surrounding plain. Tensions between the brothers, which had always simmered, began to boil over, but Roger had no choice but to obey. By Christmas he had returned to Italy with the last of his troops and was summoned to Guiscard's court. There to his astonishment he was greeted by the long-lost Judith.

Roger and Judith were a rare love story in an age of political unions. Judith's father was a powerful and ambitious noble who was determined to use his daughter to increase his connections. But Judith was in love, and had cleverly escaped him by joining a convent. There she was free from the attentions of better-qualified suitors, and had waited patiently for five years. By that time her father had quarreled with Duke William and been forced to flee Normandy, taking his daughter with him. When they arrived in Italy, Judith eagerly renounced her vows and headed straight for Guiscard's court.

After their joyful reunion, Roger proposed to marry her immediately and the humbled father gave his permission. This, however, brought up a rather embarrassing fact. Roger was about to marry into one of the great families of Normandy but didn't have any land to give her as a dowry. He had plenty of wealth – his recent campaign had provided that – but Guiscard had refused to grant him any territory. The problem was that the older brother was jealous. He had had to fight for everything he owned; his early time in Italy had been ferociously difficult, and now his little brother was expecting him to just hand over some land. There was more than just petty resentment in this. Land – and its accompanying revenue – would allow Roger to have an independent source of power aside from Guiscard's control, and turn him into a potential threat.

But Roger was no longer the inexperienced youth who had entered his brother's service, and could no longer be brushed off. He sent a formal request for land to Guiscard along with a notice that he had forty days to respond before Roger would resort to force. The older brother wasn't amused. Gathering his army, he marched into Calabria. Roger was ready for him and the two sides were soon rampaging back and forth through the countryside. Guiscard managed to trap his brother inside a town, but when he demanded entrance, the villagers sided with Roger and slammed the gates shut in his face. At this point Guiscard realized that ravaging his own territory was counterproductive, so he attempted to end the war by trickery instead of force.

He had supporters inside the town, and if he could make contact with them there was the chance to undermine Roger from within. He managed to slip inside and meet with his partisans, but the plan backfired when some passersby recognized him. Guiscard was nearly killed immediately, only managing to save his skin through a mixture of bluffs, threats, and pleading. Considerably worse for wear – but alive – he was hauled in front of Roger.

It must have been gratifying for the younger brother to sit in judgment of the older for once, but Roger was too shrewd to give vent to his frustrations. They needed each other and no petty feelings of revenge could trump their pragmatism. Roger may have taken his time to let Guiscard feel the pressure, but that was every bit as much public theater as what came next. When Guiscard was brought before his brother1, Roger publicly embraced him, weeping loudly and promising to never let such enmity come between them again. Guiscard, for his part understood the lesson perfectly. The two never quarreled again.

The settlement gave Roger some breathing room in Sicily, but unfortunately the family penchant for rivalries spilled over into the next generation. The moment Guiscard died his sons started feuding and once again it was up to Roger, now the elder statesman, to hold the splintering family together. In between battles with Muslim opponents, he had to periodically return to Italy to sort out the latest fratricidal mess, a nuisance that slowed down his conquest of Sicily considerably.

During his many excursions to Italy, Roger usually left his illegitimate son, Jordan, in charge of the Sicilian operations. The boy had clearly inherited some of the élan of his uncle, because even at a young age he combined a mix of guile and brute force to keep the conquest going. He captured one city by stealing its livestock and another by luring its citizens outside, then appearing calmly with his knights to demand the surrender. All this success, however, tempted him to try for more. His illicit birth excluded him from the succession, and in his mind that meant that he had to carve out his own dominion. When Roger returned from patching up yet another tenuous truce in Italy, he found Jordan leading a full-scale revolt to claim what he saw as his patrimony.

The irony was that Jordan was Roger's favorite son, and he would almost certainly have been left with a generous inheritance. Familial peace, however, seemed always just beyond Roger's grasp. After ruthlessly suppressing Jordan's revolt, he restored him to full favor only to see him die of a fever a few months later.

While Roger had been distracted with family issues, the situation in Sicily had deteriorated around him. Not only had his ally Ibn Timnah been assassinated, which was not such a great loss since Roger never intended to share power, but far more seriously the local populations no longer viewed the Normans as liberators. Of course Roger had only himself to blame for this latter development, as his policy of intimidation was useful for enriching himself but terrible at building loyalty. The area he had conquered was full of potential Orthodox Christian supporters, but he had been too busy extorting money to cultivate local support.

A lesson in the importance of maintaining good relations with the native populations was learned the hard way. Roger returned to his base in northeastern Sicily to begin campaigning, pausing only long enough to appropriate a local palace for his new wife. The moment he departed with his army, the Greeks of the town made common cause with the Muslims and rose up en masse. Judith somehow managed to fight her way through the streets and made it to the safety of a nearby castle. The next day Roger returned, but the opposition was so fierce that he was only able to join his bride instead of freeing her.

That winter was a particularly cold one, and although he had plenty of food, Roger was soon seriously short of fuel and warm clothing. Finally, in the early months of the next year, they found a way out. Their besiegers had access to the town's wine supply which they were consuming to stay warm. As time went by their discipline started to slip until one particularly cold night they got blindingly drunk and neglected to post a single guard. That night Roger and his soldiers managed to slip into their camp and slaughter the Muslims as they slept.

Both sides were chastened by the experience, and Roger never forgot the lesson. From that day he scrupulously courted all of his subjects regardless of their faith or ethnicity. It was good that he did so, because the North African Muslims were now on the offensive. The Islamic ruler of the coastal African city of Mahdia was determined to reassert his authority over Sicily, and he sent two armies under the command of his sons to crush the Norman upstarts. They marched inland and met Roger just west of Troina in a town called Cerami. The odds were hopelessly stacked against him. The Saracen army numbered thirty-five thousand against which he could only muster a hundred and thirty knights and three hundred foot soldiers. But the Normans had an unshakable confidence, and since Roger had situated himself on top of a hill, they had the better position. For three days the Muslim army waited for the Normans to come down. On the fourth day their patience ran out and they charged up the slope, eager to come to grips. The battle was furiously contested and lasted all day, but in the end the Norman's superior discipline prevailed. Repeated charges failed to break their line, and the hours of charging uphill had exhausted the Muslims. When they withdrew, the Normans finally came down after them, turning an ordered retreat into a rout. By nightfall the Muslim camp and baggage was in Norman hands, and the Saracen army was hopelessly shattered.

It had been one of the most extraordinary battles in history. A tiny force had not only fended off an army seventy times its size, but it had also decisively beaten it. If there was any doubt about the superiority of Norman arms before, there was none now. Despite still controlling three-quarters of Sicily, Muslim resistance was effectively broken. They would never again be on the offensive or offer a unified defense. From that moment on, the final conquest was only a matter of time.

Exactly how much time, however, was unclear. Roger followed up the victory with an attempt to take Palermo and deal the knockout blow, but the effort was a fiasco. Palermo was the third largest city in the Mediterranean with a population of a quarter of a million – only Constantinople and Cairo were bigger – and it would need a sizable army to conquer. Roger managed to talk Guiscard into providing the needed firepower, but the city still had access to the sea, making a land siege useless. Even worse, the campsite Roger chose was infested by tarantulas, whose appearance and painful bite did a thorough job of undermining everyone's morale. After only three months they cut their losses and withdrew, determined not to return until they had a fleet.

Guiscard returned to Italy to make the necessary arrangements but was delayed for seven years putting down revolts and fending off a major Byzantine attack. In the meantime, Roger exploited the old struggle of Berber vs. Arab to keep his enemies on their heels. He had learned patience from his chronic manpower shortage, and was content to slowly advance while consolidating his conquests. In 1068, the remaining Berber forces on the island managed to ambush him while he was out raiding, demanding his surrender in the face of overwhelming force. To their surprise he cheerfully opted to attack instead, smashing their army with a series of cavalry charges.

The Muslims hadn't risked an open battle with him for a while, and Roger made full use of his victory by engaging in a little psychological warfare. He had messages detailing the results of the battle written with the blood of his fallen enemies and had them sent by carrier pigeon to Palermo. When he followed it up with his army, backed up by Guiscard's long-awaited fleet, the city surrendered almost immediately.

The terms Roger offered showed just how much he had learned since the revolt of Troina. Palermo was obliged to accept the usual Norman castle, but its Muslims were free to practice their religion as long as they recognized the authority of the state. This commonsense solution, the tolerance of the outnumbered, was the cornerstone of Norman rule. It was a slow and agonizing process; the full conquest took an additional two decades, but Roger extended the same offer wherever he went. The Greek population had its churches rebuilt and refurbished at state expense, and the Muslim population, still eighty percent of Sicilians, was allowed to live and worship where it had done so for a century. The local governments, tasked with collecting taxes and enforcing justice, were kept in place, absorbing both Orthodox and Muslim into the new administration.

The only serious resistance left was from the Emir of Syracuse, the major city of Sicily's southeastern coast, but Roger would have to confront him on his own. After Palermo fell, Guiscard left the island, never to return, taking a large part of the army with him.

The first step in taking Syracuse was to make sure it was cut off from North Africa. There were still Berber troops scattered around Sicily and the Emir of Mahdia was making ominous noises. But he had been cut off from the interior of North Africa by civil war and badly needed Sicily's wheat. Roger, well aware of his difficulties, cleverly neutralized him by offering to supply Mahdia with all the food he wanted through an exclusive trading contract.

The Emir of Syracuse struck back by raiding a convent in Roger's territory and placing several of the captured nuns in his harem. This threatened to set off a religious war – something Roger wanted to avoid at all costs – and he acted at once. Raising the largest army he had ever mustered, he sent his fleet to blockade the city by sea and marched overland. The fleet arrived first and engaged the Muslim ships in the same waters where fifteen centuries before the Athenian navy had been defeated during the Peloponnesian War. The struggle this time was just as decisive. The emir took personal command of his ships but had the misfortune to fall overboard. Before his startled sailors could attempt a rescue, the heavy armor had pulled him straight to the bottom. Syracuse resisted for a few days, but without its emir it didn't have the heart for a real struggle and surrendered.

The victory virtually extinguished Muslim power in Sicily. There were still remnants to be mopped up, but by now both sides realized the end was in sight. For the better part of the next three decades Roger relentlessly pressed on and by the spring of 1086 only the single emir Ibn Hamud was left to oppose him. He was based at Agrigento on the southwestern coast, but his power stemmed from an impregnable fortress at Enna in the center of the island. Both Roger and Robert Guiscard had failed to take this citadel, and it was clear that with the limited resources available, another frontal assault wouldn't work. But there were more ways to overcome opposition than brute force, and Roger soon thought of one. As usual he prepared the ground carefully. The first step was to isolate Ibn Hamud from any possible allies. The Sicilian Muslims had traditionally received help from North Africa, but Roger managed to conclude an alliance with the Emir of Tunis, effectively cutting them off. Just after Roger's diplomats returned with news of the triumph, another messenger informed him that one of his raiding parties had managed to capture the emir's wife and children.

The only thing left to do was to plan the final coup de grace of Muslim Sicily. Robert Guiscard would undoubtedly have pressed home his advantage, storming Enna while Ibn Hamud was still reeling from his loss, but Roger had a more subtle strategy in mind. He was fully aware of the important card he now held and was careful to treat his prisoners with considerable respect. They traveled in comfort, sat at positions of honor at his table, and were granted every request short of their freedom. He deliberately took his time, rebuilding fortifications and consolidating the Norman grip over newly won territory. Ibn Hamud was left alone to meditate on the pointlessness of further resistance.

It didn't take long for the realities of the situation to sink in. The Muslim position was daily becoming more untenable, and there was no longer any hope of outside help. Thanks to Roger's mild dealings with those he conquered, it was hard for the emir to whip up much enthusiasm against him, or inspire his remaining troops to continue sacrificing for a doomed cause.

In the early months of 1087, Roger decided that the moment was right to make an offer. Accompanied by an escort of only a hundred knights, he rode to the foot of the great fortress of Enna and invited his rival to a parley. By this time the emir was visibly wavering and thanks to Roger's generous treatment of his captive family, he had privately decided to come to some accommodation with the Normans. The two of them chatted amiably enough but when the talk turned to surrender the emir sorrowfully informed his rival that it would be an unacceptable breach of his honor. Even if he were the sort of man to cast aside his integrity, he continued, his men would never accept such a cowardly act and would kill him before he could open the fortress.

Roger was astute enough to read between the lines, and he proposed an ingenious solution that would allow his rival to save face. A few days later the emir led the greater part of his forces into a carefully prepared ambush. To preserve his men's lives he nobly offered to surrender, and Enna was captured without a casualty.

Ibn Hamud gratefully had himself baptized and was offered extensive estates of his own choosing. He selected Calabria, far away from his old center of power where any revolt would make him look guilty of sedition, and was enrolled as part of the nobility. The irregularities of his past life were discreetly overlooked (he was married to his cousin) and he lived out his life in peace without incident, a perfectly respectable member of the minor aristocracy.

Roger lived for thirteen more years, streamlining his government and extending his influence to the Italian peninsula. For the most part he concentrated on increasing the prosperity of his subjects and refused to be drawn into any larger struggles[2]. When the call came for the First Crusade he was virtually the only great prince who didn't respond. Heavily outnumbered by Muslims in his own territory and dependent on trade with North Africa for wealth, the last thing he wanted was a religious war. He remained officially neutral and pressured his Muslim trading partners to be neutral as well, which turned out to be a sound economic policy. By the turn of the century Sicily was more stable, prosperous, and secure than it had ever been. Trade flourished, and the arts were blossoming. Thanks to the Crusading movement the trade of Europe and the Levant flowed through the markets of Palermo and Messina, greatly enriching all involved.

Roger's only regret was that his beloved Judith wasn't around to enjoy it with him. She had died in 1080 after presenting her husband with four daughters. A second marriage had produced three more girls along with two sons, before the second wife died as well. Roger was now in his sixties and feeling his age. His most pressing concern, as with all responsible rulers, was who would follow him.

The two legitimate sons clearly wouldn't. The first didn't survive childhood and the second had leprosy. There was an illegitimate son named Jordan who had proved to be a dashing commander in several of his father's campaigns, but he died of a fever in 1092. That year Roger married for the third time, and his new wife Adelaide[3] safely delivered two sons. The oldest was named Simon and the younger Roger after his happy father, who could now rest assured that his name would be continued. Six years later Roger expired peacefully in his bed, having ruled wisely and well. His military victories had been legendary, but it was his administration that had been truly brilliant. He was that most rare leader, one who not only knew how to conquer, but more importantly how to rule. He had been only twenty-six when he entered Sicily, a young, ambitious knight seeking his fortune, and forty-four years later he had expired as the great statesman of the Mediterranean. His genius as an administrator is still remembered fondly by

Sicilians today, who gave him the nickname 'The Great Count'.

Roger's final gift for Sicily was only apparent after he was gone. Strong rulers can leave uncertainty and disorder in their wake, but Roger had devoted his life to good government and it continued without him. His younger son and eventual successor, Roger II, was only five years old at his death, and although long minorities often lead to chaos, he ascended twelve years later without opposition to a calm and stable kingdom. Few rulers have left a finer legacy.

Chapter Thirteen

ROGERIOS REX

The stability of the Sicilian government immediately after Count Roger died was surprising partially because the Hautevilles were unusually prolific. In addition to his sons Roger had had at least twelve daughters, which meant a dozen son-in-laws potentially fighting over the succession. It would not have been difficult to wrest control from either of Roger's sons. The older one, Simon, was only eight when his father died, and although he was dutifully proclaimed Count of Sicily and Calabria, real power was held by his mother, Adelaide.

To an outsider looking in, this was a disaster waiting to happen. Adelaide was completely alienated from the people she ruled. She was from the north of Italy – vastly different from these southerners – struggled with Latin, spoke only a touch of French, and had no Arabic or Greek at all. To her, the Norman barons must have seemed almost as alien as the Sicilians, forever quarreling and only cowed by a more dominant personality. For anyone to impose their will, much less a foreign woman, must have seemed a hopeless task.

But somehow, Adelaide was able to do it. Not merely to hold her own, although that would have been accomplishment enough, but to provide a stable and peaceful regency for her sons. The surviving accounts gloss over her methods, but

Adelaide deserves to be remembered as one of the unsung heroes of Norman Sicily.

Her tenure wasn't without its challenges. Young Simon died after only four years and Adelaide took the most important step of her regency by moving the government from Messina to the great trading city of Palermo. There she had the ten-year-old Roger II knighted and raised him among a mix of Italian, Arab, Greek, and Lombard courtiers. The change could be seen throughout the rest of young Roger's life. The men who had created his world – Count Roger, Robert Guiscard, and William Iron-Arm – had been Norman through and through. Roger II, growing up without a father in the most cosmopolitan city in Western Europe, was something new: a Sicilian.

When he turned sixteen, his mother decided that he had come of age. The economy was booming thanks to the success of the First Crusade and the immense volume of trade that now flooded through Sicilian markets. There seemed little point in holding Roger back; she had raised him to be a leader and it was time to step aside. But she was also motivated by new plans of her own. Baldwin, the king of Jerusalem, had recently put aside his wife and was actively courting Adelaide (or, more accurately, the money and soldiers she would bring with her). In the spring of that year he had sent emissaries to Palermo and rashly told them to agree to any demands she might have. As expected, she drove a hard bargain. Baldwin was childless and Adelaide, as always looking after the interests of her son, stipulated that if it remained that way Roger II would inherit Jerusalem on her death. With great pomp befitting a woman of her station, she boarded a ship for the Levant and a new age for Sicily began.

Roger II was wealthy and secure, but like any of his ambitious ancestors he wanted to turn that money into military strength.

The most practical way of doing this on an island was to build up a navy and he was fortunate to have a gifted civil servant at his disposal. The man's name was Christodulus, and Roger, recognizing his abilities, created a new title to reflect his status as the highest member of the navy. He Latinized the Arab word 'emir' to 'ammiratus', and created the first admiral in history.

Christodulus didn't disappoint. He produced a well-trained navy that was easily the finest in the western Mediterranean. Roger II just needed an excuse to use it and one was helpfully provided almost immediately. The city of Mahdia in North Africa had been a major trading partner for Sicilian ports from the days when the Arabs controlled the island, and the resulting wealth had allowed it to control much of the surrounding coast. This dominance had earned Mahdia plenty of enemies and when one of them was given a friendly audience in Palermo, the Emir of Mahdia responded by raiding Roger's territory in Calabria. Even by the standards of the time the brutality was unexpected. The town of Nicotera was wiped off the map. Its women were raped, its men and children were slaughtered, and everything of value that wasn't nailed down was carried off to the waiting ships. As a final warning the entire town was then burned to the ground.

This was more than just a simple raid; it struck at the heart of medieval authority. The loyalty of a people to their lord was directly proportionate to his ability to protect them. To leave the strike unavenged for too long was to risk a serious erosion of his power. There was also a threat from his barons. None would confront him directly, but they would be happy to exploit the disaster for their own ends. If the people of Calabria didn't feel protected by Palermo they would switch their allegiance to one of the closer nobility. Christodulus was ordered to sail for Mahdia at once.

The situation in North Africa looked increasingly promising every day. The Emir of Mahdia died and although his fourteen-year-old son managed to hang on to the city, the region dissolved into chaos as petty strongmen tried to settle old scores and seize control. As Christodulus approached, not a single Saracen ship appeared to contest the landing. Just as it appeared that the Normans would have an easy victory, however, their luck deserted them. A violent storm drove them ten miles off course, forcing them to seek shelter on some sandy islands off the coast. The next morning Christodulus left to scout out the strength of Mahdia's defenses, and while he was gone a Muslim force discovered his camp and sacked it. The dispirited Normans tried to salvage the situation by seizing a castle on the coast but instead of cowing the Mahdians it had the opposite effect. The squabbling North Africans now had a common enemy, and when the young emir declared a jihad they all responded. Most of the Normans managed to make it back to their ships, but those that were left behind were slaughtered to a man. Christodulus had no choice; he cut his losses and headed back to Palermo, but even then his tribulations weren't over. On the voyage home another storm hit and barely a third of those who had set out managed to return home.

Roger's first youthful flexing of power had been painfully rebuffed, and the loss of prestige that he suffered was enormous. Not only had he refused to lead the raid in person, which was enough to raise eyebrows among the barons of his father's generation, but his vaunted navy had been bested by a fourteen-year-old. There was immediate pressure to find a scapegoat and Christodulus was a natural one, but to his credit Roger refused. There were no reprisals or purges. He would never forget the humiliation, but he was a patient man.

Revenge would come, but it would arrive at a time of Roger's choosing and not a moment before.

In the meantime there were more promising opportunities in Italy. The entire south was in chaos. Roger's formidable uncle Guiscard had ruled with an iron hand, but his son Roger Borsa had been too weak to impose his will on the stubborn barons. When Borsa had died, he had been followed in turn by his even less competent son William. By 1121, Calabria was completely lawless and William, who was chronically short of money, had little authority beyond the walls of his own castle. Roger wasn't above a little opportunistic grabbing and he invited his cousin to a lavish banquet. After casually displaying his wealth with an impressive feast, Roger dangled the prospect of financial aid in return for being named heir to William's territory. This was eagerly agreed to and Roger withdrew to Palermo to wait out events.

In the meantime he turned his attention to Malta. His father had invaded the island and forced its Arab masters to pay tribute, but Roger wasn't comfortable having an area so close to Sicily under Muslim control. In 1127 he sent his refurbished navy to end the threat once and for all. This time the naval operation was commanded by a young Byzantine, George of Antioch.

As a teenager, George had left Asia Minor and moved to North Africa where he gained employment with the Muslim rulers of Mahdia. He fell out of favor with the emir's son and decided to defect to Sicily on the eve of the Norman invasion. To make good his escape he waited until the Arabs were at their Friday prayers, then disguised himself as a sailor and managed to slip aboard a merchant ship. When he arrived in Palermo he marched up to the palace and asked for a job. His boldness paid off. Roger, always a good judge of character, saw immediately the usefulness of a man who was an expert in both the language and politics of North Africa. He was appointed as Christodulus's second-in-command and in the years after the Mahdia expedition he increasingly outshone his superior.

The expedition to Malta was carried off flawlessly, a foretaste of the triumphs that lay in store. The Muslims were expelled and the island was added to Roger's growing domain. George's return to Palermo was greeted with celebration, and even better news followed on its heels. In Calabria, Roger's cousin William had suddenly died and, as promised, Roger stood to inherit his lands.

The trouble was that William, like many weak rulers before him, had made the same promise to a number of people – including the pope. The only point everyone could agree on was that Roger shouldn't get a thing. The idea of a single figure controlling all of southern Italy and Sicily was the stuff of papal nightmares and the Norman barons of Italy had no desire to exchange the freedoms to which they had grown accustomed for a strong central authority. Roger had to act quickly before his enemies had a chance to organize themselves.

To start the offensive he sent George of Antioch to seize the port of Salerno. The city was ready for him and had the gates shut tight, so the admiral sailed his fleet back and forth in full view of the walls for ten days. The silent procession unnerved the defenders. The last time Salerno had resisted a Norman it had been Guiscard at the walls, and he had shown no mercy when he finally managed to enter. The Salernians weren't ready to tempt fate again. Figuring it was better to come to terms with a determined Hauteville while he was still in the mood to make an offer, they surrendered.

Guiscard probably would still have executed a few leading citizens for daring to hold out ten days, but when it came to

war, Roger was more Byzantine than Norman. Diplomatic
victories were the kind he liked best; they left his army completely intact and didn't wreck the governmental machinery
of the conquered place. After installing a small garrison, Roger
hurried inland to capture Benevento. When he arrived he was
pleasantly surprised to find his chief rival the pope with only a
small retinue. Leaving a besieging force to keep him occupied,
Roger took his army on a leisurely tour of southern Italy, mop-
ping up all resistance. Like Salerno, this was largely a bloodless
campaign. The rebellious barons were too fractured to band
together and not foolish enough to engage Roger alone. Some
of them made a show of resistance but inevitably they all cut
their losses and swore to accept Roger as their feudal lord.

The only holdout now was the pope, and although he was
too independent to give up so easily, he couldn't do much
mischief while cooped up in Benevento. So Roger, who never
liked to be gone from Palermo for too long, returned to his
capital well satisfied with his work.

Victory celebrations, however, were premature. The
moment Roger's army departed, the barons had second
thoughts about their oaths, and the pope, who had managed
to escape from Benevento, found it easy to rally them into
an immense anti-Sicilian league. Just two months after the
nobility of southern Italy had pledged oaths of fealty to Roger,
they were down on one knee again, promising not to rest until
all of Roger's agents were thrown out of the peninsula.

Despite the obvious danger, Roger acted with deliberate
calmness, taking time to gather his army and make his way
through the heel of Italy where his support was strongest.
His wealth gave him a great advantage. Unlike his opponents
he could afford to keep a large army in the field almost
indefinitely. But his greatest weapon was time. He knew that if

he was patient enough to not force a major battle, the hot sun and restless nature of feudal[1] levies would do the rest.

The pope, meanwhile, was beginning to discover that his allies were impossible to control. The independent streak that had led them to revolt also made them incapable of working together, and they were constantly threatening to withdraw from the league. With each day that passed without action, the grand papal army disintegrated a little more.

As the weeks dragged by Roger refused to deviate from this tactic. Even when the two armies ran into each other – the vanguard of the papal army stumbled into the Norman line while it was crossing a river – Roger merely withdrew to higher ground and waited. For the entire month of July both sides stared at each other as the summer sun beat down. Tempers flared as the feudal levies, who had no use for sitting around, grumbled and the barons started quarreling about what their next move should be. By August, with his army shrinking, the pope was having second thoughts. This alliance was too unstable and exhausting to maintain, and in any case Roger, whose own camp looked depressingly disciplined and orderly, was too powerful to crush. Perhaps the better strategy would be to embrace the Normans. A strong ruler was a potential threat that every pope since William Iron-Arm's day had tried to avoid in southern Italy, but the peninsula needed peace, and the danger of an over-mighty ruler was preferable to the current chaos. Besides, these stubborn barons were impossible – let them be Roger's problem.

The pope withdrew and sent a messenger to the Norman camp saying that he was willing to officially recognize Roger's claims to southern Italy. Without their papal sponsor holding them together the rebellious barons melted away, and the levies dissolved. Roger had managed to defeat his enemies without engaging in a single pitched battle.

The pope's one attempt to salvage his dignity was to insist that the ceremony formally investing Roger with his cousin's territory not be held on papal territory. So, on the evening of August 22, 1128 he met Count Roger on a bridge outside of Benevento. In the presence of twenty thousand spectators, each carrying a torch, he elevated him to Duke of Apulia, Calabria, and Sicily.

The Norman barons present, as the pope had suspected, were not impressed with their new feudal lord. No one doubted Roger's intelligence – his recent campaign was proof enough of that – but he had shown a reluctance to fight that didn't sit well with the warlike Normans. Waiting for an enemy to fall apart seemed somehow cowardly; Norman respect was won on the battlefield.

By nature these men hated central authority. They would bow down to Roger's armies, but the moment he was gone they would rise up again in revolt. Even the formidable Guiscard had never really managed to change that. Almost as if to prove that point, even as Roger was receiving his new title, another revolt was already underway.

It took a year to put down in a mostly bloodless campaign. Roger picked off the barons one by one, taking his time to make sure that the country was pacified before moving on. When the last one had surrendered, he surprised them all by offering generous pardons, and called a vast assembly of all the nobles and clergy of southern Italy and Sicily. He had thought long and hard about how to solve the structural instability of the Norman lands, how to break the feuding tribal society that had evolved over the last century, and had come up with an ingenious combination of propaganda and law to wield the patchwork of territories into a single state.

The entire assembly, clergy and nobles alike, were treated to a glittering display of ducal wealth, and then made to swear new oaths to Roger and his two sons. All the old promises were repeated – to respect the duke and his property – and a new one was added. The nobility had mistaken Roger's diplomacy and pardons for softness, and now they discovered that there was iron underneath the velvet. Each of them was forced to swear not to engage in private warfare, to allow no acts of lawlessness on their lands, and to surrender all brigands to the duke's justice. To ensure this last part (Roger knew better than to trust their honor) he gave his courts teeth. If any noble failed to comply, they would be hunted down like a common criminal. The traditional way of life of the Normans since they had come to Italy, the 'right of feud' had abruptly come to an end. From now on the nobility, like the peasants they controlled, were bound by the rule of law. This was the most significant development in southern Italy since the coming of the Normans themselves.

Most, no doubt, hoped that it was only a phase that would pass as soon as Roger returned to Sicily, but he was in deadly earnest. On every public occasion for the rest of his long reign he had those oaths repeated and renewed lest any of his nobles should be tempted to forget.

Roger was now thirty-two and had accomplished more than any Norman since Guiscard. Against stiff papal and local resistance he had united all Norman lands in Italy, and had tighter control over the area than Guiscard had ever managed. But like any good Hauteville, he had bigger dreams. For all intents he already had a kingdom; now he wanted a crown.

There was no chance that the current pope would agree to any such thing, but fortunately for Roger the pope died the following year. The expected successor was a popular cardinal of Jewish descent who took the name Anacletus II, but before his supporters had a chance to organize, a group of rival cardinals hastily elected a reformer named Innocent. The outraged cardinals, who made up a majority of the electing body, went ahead and installed Anacletus anyway, and for a few months there were rival camps in Rome each claiming that the other pope was illegitimate.

Anacletus, whose family was very wealthy and had made frequent donations to public entertainment, was far more popular than Innocent, and a few armed street fights between the sides convinced Innocent of that fact. He fled from Rome to France where he pleasantly discovered that the situation was reversed. Thanks to the reform movement that was sweeping through western Europe, the exiled pope found himself a cause célèbre. No one outside of Italy had any desire to return to the bad old corrupt days when the papacy was the plaything of Roman aristocrats, and the well-connected Anacletus seemed to promise just that. The most respected voice in Christendom, Bernard of Clairvaux[2], took up Innocent's cause. Bernard, a seemingly minor abbot of a small French monastery, dominated all of Europe for nearly two decades through the sheer force of his personality. The result of his championing of Innocent's cause was that the kings of France and England – as well as the German emperor – hurried to pledge their support.

Anacletus, who had paraded through the streets of Rome in triumph just a few months before, now suddenly found virtually all of Christendom united against him. Terrified, he turned to the one power which had characteristically not declared for either side – Sicily.

Roger's only condition, equally predictably, was that Anacletus give him a crown. Apulia, Calabria, and Sicily were still vastly different places and he needed the mystique of royalty to bind them together. The pope wasn't in a position to argue and both sides knew it. After a modest show of contemplation, he agreed without reservation.

Roger, however, was careful to stage the coronation in a way that made it clear that his crown was not at the whim of a pope. The title of king may have been granted by a pontiff, but it could not be taken away by another occupant of St Peter's throne. A mass meeting of the important nobles, abbots, and bishops was called and he formally presented them with his argument for being elevated to king. Sicily, he claimed, had once been the seat of an ancient kingdom and therefore this was not a new creation bestowed by the pope, but a restoration. The assembled nobles agreed unanimously by loud acclamation and the meeting broke up. Roger could now claim that the people had urged him to become king; there would be no whiff of the charge of usurpation. As always, he drove this point home with official propaganda. A mosaic was commissioned showing him receiving the crown not from the pope, but from Christ himself.

The ceremony took place on Christmas Day 1130 in Palermo, and anybody who was anybody tried to cram into the city. The nobility competed to outdo each other with ostentatious displays of wealth, and the locals hung silks and threw flowers from every balcony and upper window. It was, as one eyewitness put it, as if the whole city was being crowned. As was fitting, Roger himself outshone them all. Dressed in a cloth of red and gold he presided over a vast banquet. The servants were dressed in finer silks than many of the watching nobility, and the food was served on settings of silver and gold.

When it was finished, he processed to Palermo's cathedral and stood before the high altar for a service almost unique in Christian history. The Catholic archbishop of Palermo presided, with Greek Orthodox priests attending, and the pope's representative held the holy oil. Roger knelt and was anointed with sacred oil, and then his chief vassal placed the crown on his head. When it was over he stood, and the great doors were thrown open to Palermo's population.

Sicily had been a witness to most of the great Mediterranean empires. The Carthaginians, Romans, Byzantines, and Arabs had in turn ruled over the island. But for all of these it had been a mere conquered province exploited for its grain, forever passed between more powerful neighbors and considered important only for what resources it could provide distant capitals. Now, for the first time in its long history (despite the claims of Roger to the contrary) it had a king of its own, and on that Christmas Day in 1130 the citizens of Palermo caught their first splendid glimpse of him.

Roger's crown, however well earned, had come with a fearsome cost. To get it he had backed an antipope and defied the rest of Christendom. At the time, of course, it wasn't clear which of the rival popes, Anacletus or Innocent, would emerge the victor, but as the months passed more and more crowned heads moved to Innocent's camp.

This was largely due to the influence of the tireless Bernard of Clairvaux who convinced both the wavering French king and Henry I of England – along with the majority of the population outside of Italy – to support Innocent. The one important holdout was the German king Lothair who was being heavily courted by both sides. As far as the German was concerned, Anacletus' great advantage was that he controlled Rome. Lothair could only be crowned emperor in the eternal city, and he wouldn't be completely secure on his own throne until that was done. Since popular opinion was clearly on Innocent's side he waffled as long as possible until a personal visit by Bernard changed his mind. Poor Lothair tried to resist, but a public tongue-lashing soon had him promising to lead an army down to Rome to evict Anacletus, overthrow Roger, and install Innocent.

When Lothair finally arrived in Italy in the spring of 1133, he found the situation unexpectedly in his favor. Roger's coronation was deeply unpopular in southern Italy. The great Norman barons of the peninsula saw no reason why they should have their wings clipped by a man whose family had only been there for a generation, and in anticipation of Lothair's arrival they had gathered a rebel army and stormed several royal castles. Roger, in a rare miscalculation, had taken the field against them. He had shown great personal valor, cutting a swath through the opposing infantry, but his own army had been smashed. The defeat shook even his closest supporters. Venosa, the bastion of Hauteville power where four of the most famous members of his family lay buried in state, joined the rebels. Across Apulia and Calabria royal garrisons were slaughtered, and men flocked to the imperial banner. The long-dreaded clash between empire and island kingdom was at hand.

Roger was clearly the weaker of the two, but he kept his head. The size and speed of the rebellion had taken Lothair by surprise as well, and he wasn't prepared to take full advantage of it. When the rebel leaders met with him they were disappointed to find that the size of his army had been greatly exaggerated. He had only brought with him some two thousand men, hardly enough to capture Rome or topple Roger from his new throne.

Lothair had expected his presence to be enough to rattle Anacletus, but instead he dug in his heels. The Norman-supported pope and his supporters controlled the right bank of the Tiber including the fortress of Castel San'Angelo and St Peter's, and refused to budge. The German king had to settle for installing Innocent into the older Lateran Palace where he was dutifully crowned emperor while being taunted by Anacletus' supporters across the Tiber.

The newly-minted emperor proved a grave disappointment to his Italian allies. Any hopes that he would stay to lead a grand offensive against Roger were dashed a few days after the ceremony. Lothair had pressing business in Germany and had obtained what he wanted from Italy. Making a promise to return in force, more as a sop to Bernard than a serious pledge, he withdrew over the Alps as quickly as he could.

His departure left the rebels stranded. Roger had rebuilt his army and was in no mood to show them any mercy. Innocent tried to assist the barons as much as he could by excommunicating any soldier who participated in Roger's army, but the clever Sicilian had recruited his troops from the island's Muslims who couldn't care less about the pope. Every major rebellious town in Apulia was burnt and its leaders executed. Roger had customarily shown generosity in victory but now there was only the mailed fist. The two barons who had started the rebellion were rounded up and publicly humiliated. The first was hung while the second was made to hold the rope, then he too was dispatched. Roger returned to Sicily well pleased with himself. Despite the disastrous start to the year it had ended in triumph. His papal candidate was still secure in Rome, his entire kingdom was at peace, and he had successfully defied the emperor.

Unfortunately it proved to be only a short respite. Within a few weeks of his return to Palermo a fever swept through the city, leaving the queen dead and Roger broken with grief. He shut himself up in the palace, refusing to see anyone, and the resulting rumor that he was dead awoke all the rebellious dreams in southern Italy. More serious still was the news from the North.

Lothair had been quite pleased with his Italian adventure. He had technically fulfilled his oath to install Innocent as pope in Rome, and had gotten his crown. Unfortunately for him, however, Bernard of Clairvaux wasn't amused by his half-hearted performance. The abbot had come to the sensible conclusion that Anacletus would never be ousted from Rome while Roger was king of Sicily, so he demanded that Lothair turn around, re-invade Italy, and properly finish the job.

Bernard wasn't the only one worried about Roger. Southern Italy had been at least partly under control of the Byzantine Empire for the better part of the last thousand years and now the Sicilians had started raiding Byzantium's rich Dalmatian coast. How long before Roger had the same idea as his uncle Guiscard and invaded the imperial homeland? The Byzantine emperor John the Beautiful didn't want to wait around and find out. He wrote to Lothair offering his support in a joint attack on Sicily.

The Byzantine ambassador found a second ally when he stopped by Venice on his way to Germany. The Venetian trading empire had been considerably hurt by the growth of Palermo and the Doge offered the full support of his navy.

In Germany, the situation had also considerably improved for Lothair since his coronation. The imperial crown had cowed his potential rivals and he could now afford to throw all of his considerable resources into an Italian campaign. He spent a year gathering his forces, and when the snows cleared he crossed the Alps and descended into northern Italy.

This time there was no resisting the Germans. The northern cities fell with barely a struggle and the Norman barons again rose up in revolt. Pope Innocent, together with his court, joined Lothair as the emperor received the submission of the Italian cities. With any luck they would mop up the mainland before winter hit and the following spring invade Sicily.

Despite the seriousness of the threat to his kingdom, Roger didn't panic. He had two great advantages: the summer heat, and the feudal underpinnings of Lothair's army. The German emperor wasn't an absolute monarch. He could command several months of military service from his vassals, but couldn't hold them forever. The longer the campaign wore on, the more restless they would become, so Roger carefully avoided any battles. Every time Lothair advanced, he retreated. At the same time, he constantly offered to meet separately with his antagonists to strain the relationship between pope and emperor.

By the late summer his efforts had paid off. The heat was oppressive, malaria had decimated the ranks, and Lothair's vassals were openly demanding to be released from service. Virtually the only thing they could all agree on was their distaste for the pope and his Italian court who complained constantly and for whose sake they had been dragged hundreds of miles from their homes. Things got so bad that there was an attempt on the pope's life[3] that was only thwarted by Lothair's personal involvement. In a last ditch effort to force a decisive battle, the emperor besieged Roger's mainland capital of Salerno, but the Sicilian king calmly stayed where he was.

The annoyed emperor told his Italian allies to look after themselves and returned across the Alps. The entire campaign had been a colossal waste of time. He hadn't managed to accomplish anything permanent, there were still two popes arguing over Rome, Roger was still as secure as ever, and without the imperial army the Italian rebels couldn't hope to stand against the Normans. When Lothair died suddenly two months after returning to Germany, the Sicilian king had already recovered most of his territory.

The emperor was followed to the grave a few months later by Roger's pope, Anacletus II. Innocent was now the rightful pontiff by default, and Roger did his best to come to terms with his old enemy. As he stamped out the last traces of revolt he was careful not to cross into papal territory. He also officially recognized Innocent as the rightful pope and sent letters to all his supporters to do likewise.

As far as Innocent was concerned, however, this was far too little too late. Without Roger's meddling he would have been the accepted pope for years now, and the Church wouldn't have had to go through the pain and embarrassment of a schism. Roger was officially excommunicated (for the second time) and, since no emperor was handy to lend an army, Innocent raised one himself and invaded the Norman kingdom.

Papal armies had never fared well against the Normans, and this one was no exception. On July 22, 1139 the forces of Innocent were ambushed by Roger as they crossed the Garigliano River. By nightfall the pope, his cardinals, and his entire treasury were all in Roger's hands. Like his predecessor Pope Leo IX who had been captured by Robert Guiscard, Innocent bore his defeat stoically. The Normans treated him with excessive respect, almost enough to disguise the fact that he was a prisoner, but he was under no illusions as to what he had to do. Three days later he officially confirmed Roger as King of Sicily, Duke of Apulia, and Prince of Capua, and recognized term by term what Anacletus had agreed to nine years before. He was powerless to do otherwise, but he did have one last spark of defiance. At the ceremony celebrating the occasion, with Roger in attendance dressed in the heavy robes of state and the summer sun beating mercilessly down, he preached a sermon of enormous length.

The return to Sicily was a happy one for Roger. Southern

Italy had finally been pacified – it was never again to offer serious resistance to him for the remainder of his reign – and he left it in the capable hands of his son Roger III. It had taken him ten years to win his kingdom against the strenuous opposition of two emperors and a pope, and now he meant to make sure it endured. The first step was to give it a constitution: uniform laws that would create a strong, centralized state. The German invasion had shown him the limitations of a feudal arrangement, so he patterned his kingdom on autocratic Byzantium. In a flurry of laws he created his idea of the divine monarchy, an all-powerful sovereign who never let the mask of authority slip. Reinforcing this was a new uniform coinage copied directly from Byzantine coins, which showed Roger in imperial robes on one side and Christ Pantocrator[4] on the reverse. The old Norman coins had displayed St Peter to show their loyalty to the pope, but the king of Sicily had a more direct connection to the divine.

Along with the internal reforms came a rash of architectural and scientific activity. The two crown jewels of Norman Sicily, the Palatine Chapel and the Martorana, were built with royal funds, each a unique fusion of Byzantine, Arab, and Norman culture. A great commission based in the busy port city of Palermo was appointed to study geography. For over a decade every ship that requested entry to Sicily was boarded and questioned about what they had seen. The geographical information collected was recorded in two places, a large globe of pure silver inscribed with the known world's continents and countries, and a thick tome called The Book of Roger.

The effort was surprisingly accurate. Scandinavia is described as having few hours of sunlight in the winter, and the sister Norman kingdom of England is described as cold and wet. It even correctly describes the earth as round some three and a half centuries before Columbus. Palermo became the center of a mini-Renaissance, the one place outside Spain or Constantinople where scholars had access to Greek, Arab, and Western learning.

During this period Roger also managed to neutralize his most outspoken critic, Bernard of Clairvaux. Before he had returned to Germany, Lothair had made it quite clear what he thought of the pope, and Bernard, a zealous guard of papal dignity, had been offended. Roger, on the other hand, was a generous patron of the Church, and his donations to the Cistercian order had swung the abbot of Clairvaux over to his side.

Byzantium and the Western Empire, however, the two other great enemies of Norman Sicily, had not forgotten their humiliations. They had left Roger in peace so far only because each power had been swept up in its own problems. Both imperial thrones suffered sudden vacancies. Just six years after Lothair expired, his Byzantine counterpart John Comnenus was killed in a freak hunting accident. The new monarchs, Conrad of Hohenstauffen in Germany and Manuel Comnenus in Constantinople, solemnly agreed to a joint campaign, but just as they mobilized their armies one of the Crusader kingdoms fell to the Turks and a new crusade erupted. The imperial relationship was severely strained when German forces marching through Byzantine territory failed to distinguish between Greeks and Turks, bringing the two empires to the brink of war.

Somehow, through it all, Conrad and Manuel managed to strike up a genuinely warm friendship. When Conrad was injured during the crusade Manuel personally nursed him back to health, and the two renewed their pledge to go to war against Roger. Two years later the imperial families got closer still when Manuel married Conrad's daughter Bertha.

The nuptials were a warning to Roger of the determination

of his enemies, and a public rebuke. He had been trying to get Manuel to marry one of his daughters for years, although frankly his behavior hadn't helped his cause. During the crusade he had taken advantage of Manuel's distraction to have his admiral George of Antioch sack Athens, Thebes, and Corinth, the three richest cities of Byzantine Greece.

The provoked Manuel raised a huge army thirty-thousand strong, but just as the long-awaited campaign was about to get underway a horde of barbarians came pouring over the Pindus Mountains into northern Greece, and the emperor was forced to divert his army to deal with the threat. Manuel was a capable general[5], but by the time he had driven the barbarians out, the snows had ended the campaigning season.

In the spring he tried again, but again was delayed. This time it was Sicilian gold that financed an uprising in the Balkans[6], threatening the empire's western border. Manuel sent the fleet to deal with the problem and while it was away Roger cheekily had his admiral sail into the waters off of the coast of Constantinople and fire some arrows into the gardens of the imperial palace.

Such delaying tactics could only last for so long. By 1152 both Conrad and Manuel had dealt with their respective obstacles and were ready to march. The two emperors made plans to meet in northern Italy and then continue south where the Venetian fleet would be waiting there to ferry them across the straits to Sicily. The moment was perfect; Roger's son and namesake had recently died and Roger, who had now outlived five of his six children, seemed suddenly old and vulnerable.

There seemed little that could save the Norman kingdom from the coming storm, but this time it was spared by luck. In the spring of 1152, just as Conrad was starting his march, he abruptly died, and as Germany convulsed in a power struggle the war against Roger was quietly abandoned. Manuel had too many enemies closer to home to risk it alone, and in any case he had already realized that Venice posed a far more serious threat than Palermo. Even now he was considering the first strike against the Sea-Republic that would lead inexorably to the tragedy of the Fourth Crusade[7].

That was some years in the future, but it already seemed as if an age was ending. Conrad was merely the first of the great figures to exit the stage. He was followed the next year by Bernard of Clairvaux and then George of Antioch, the remarkable admiral who had won the Normans their North African empire. The loss of his most able advisor seemed to sap the last of Roger's energy. He retired to his pleasure dome in Palermo, a mix of exotic zoo, garden, and palace, and died quietly two years later.

The king's body was laid to rest in a simple porphyry tomb in Palermo's cathedral, fittingly dressed in the ornate robes and drooping pearl crown of a Byzantine emperor. Across his chest was laid his sword, emblazoned in Latin with the words "The Apulian, Calabrian, Sicilian, and African all obey my will".

He had been a remarkable ruler, and Sicily was never to see one like him again. If his behavior at times left much to be desired (his infidelity was famous) he never shirked the responsibilities of kingship. He was a unique blend of northern energy and southern refinement, the product and inspiration of the Norman kingdom in full bloom. After him it would slide into dissolution, but he still possessed the fearsome drive of his ancestors that had won them two kingdoms at opposite ends of Europe. As one courtier wrote, he 'accomplished more in his sleep than others did in their waking day'.

That accomplishment had been the seemingly impossible

task of forging a petty, tribal land of diverse cultures and
religions into a single united kingdom. Compared with the
rest of the Italian peninsula, which remained stubbornly
divided and quarreling for the next seven centuries, Roger's
territory was a beacon of hope of what was possible. It was
also surprisingly enduring. It was battered and squandered,
tossed around between the crowned heads of Europe, but
the kingdom of Sicily remained intact until the unification of
modern Italy in the nineteenth century.

The great king may have been buried in the cathedral
of Cefalù in Sicily, but it is in the church of Santa Maria
dell'Ammiraglio that he is most appropriately remembered.
There, the gift he bestowed to his beloved island is enshrined
in marble and gold, a fusion of art and architecture that even
after eight centuries still manages to catch the breath.

Each of the three great civilizations of Sicily's past is
blended in this penultimate church, a fitting tribute to the
man who created Norman Sicily. Built in the traditional form
of a Greek cross, the interior drips with gold, covered by a
magnificent cycle of Byzantine mosaics depicting scenes from
the life of Christ. Beneath the Greek icons and the Norman
arches, Fatimid artisans of North Africa carved two immense
wooden doors and left a hymn to the Virgin Mary inscribed
in Arabic at the base of the main dome. Most impressive of
all is a mosaic found on an unassuming interior wall of the
nave. There the Christian king who dressed as an Arab and
decorated his church in the Byzantine and Muslim styles had
himself depicted.

It remains the only surviving likeness of Roger II that was
produced by men who had seen him, and it captures completely
the spirit of Norman Sicily. Adorned with the dalmatic and
stole of a Byzantine emperor, the 'baptized Sultan'[8] leans

forward slightly to receive his crown from the hands of Christ. Above his head simple Greek letters spell out the Latin phrase 'Rogerios Rex' – Roger the King.

It was a title he had struggled most of his adult life for, wrenching it from the unwilling grasp of no less than two opposing popes. Yet there was no statesman of the twelfth century who deserved it more. He had found an island torn apart by religious and cultural divisions and had welded it into the most prosperous and effectively run kingdom in Europe. In doing so he had provided an invaluable guide on how to govern a modern state, to unite seemingly irreconcilable parties into a strong and functioning whole. His reign was a rare oasis of peace on an otherwise turbulent medieval stage. After him, the sun began to inexorably set on the Sicilian kingdom.

Chapter Fourteen

WILLIAM THE BAD

*Dextera Domini Fecit Virtutem; Dextera Domini
Exaltavit Me*

"The Right Hand of God gave me courage; The Right
Hand of God raised me up."

– Inscription on the Great Count's sword after the Battle
of Cerami and on his grandson's Treaty of Benevento

In 1154 Roger II was succeeded by his youngest son, William, and by all outward appearances it was a splendid choice. The twenty-three-year-old was a magnificent physical specimen, a hulking throwback to his Viking ancestors, easily towering over his diminutive Mediterranean subjects. His face was dominated by a thick, black beard, and he was known for his massive strength, reportedly able to straighten an iron horseshoe with his bare hands. If, however, he loomed larger than his father physically, he had acquired little of his political skills. Much of this was Roger's own fault. It's always difficult to succeed a great man, but Roger hardly bothered to prepare his heir. He had made a point instead to constantly identify his son's shortcomings.

William was the youngest of the four boys from his first marriage, considered unlikely and unworthy to ever wear the crown. As such he was virtually ignored, given no important administrative or military office to prepare him for leadership. He grew up largely left to himself, enjoying the luxuries of the palace without any of its responsibilities. Within a single decade, though, his world was turned upside down. His older brothers unexpectedly died, and at the age of thirty he was abruptly thrust on the throne, completely unprepared.

Unsurprisingly, William was more concerned with enjoying the good life than learning statecraft. While he built ever more extravagant palaces, he left the day-to-day affairs of the kingdom to others, in most cases not even bothering to appoint new ministers but simply confirming his father's choices in their posts. The only exception he made to this general policy was to raise a young chancellor named Maio to the supreme administrative post of admiral.

It was a wise choice. Maio was the son of a judge from the southern Italian town of Bari, and had received the best classical education money could buy. In the cosmopolitan atmosphere of Palermo he more than held his own, displaying a ruthless disregard of popularity or softness. Without his iron hand, William, who was far more interested in his hunting parks than governing, would have been lucky to keep his throne for more than a few months.

The international stage had become much more dangerous since the last years of Roger II. The Byzantine and German Empires were both ruled by outstanding figures – the ferocious Frederick Barbarossa in Germany, and the smooth Manuel Comnenus in Constantinople. Fortunately for William, their mutual distrust kept them checked. At his coronation, Barbarossa had announced that he would restore the Western Empire to greatness. This meant bringing Sicily and southern Italy under his control, and since both of those territories recently belonged to the Byzantine Empire, Barbarossa considered the emperor Manuel to be his principal enemy. With this in mind he signed a treaty with the pope to exclude Byzantium from any division of the Norman kingdom. At the same time he kept up a correspondence with Manuel, dangling the idea of a mutual campaign but always finding an excuse to delay it. Manuel only discovered the deception after Barbarossa's army had already left Germany to win Italy without him.

The German monarch expected trouble in the north of Italy since anti-Imperial sentiment was always strong, but when he descended from the Alps he found the entire peninsula in a religious uproar.

Pope Adrian IV, the only Englishman ever to sit on the papal throne, was the latest in a long line of foreign, reforming popes. He had cut his teeth reorganizing the Scandinavian church, and expected to do a thorough house-cleaning of St Peter's. His entry into Rome, however, had been a rude awakening for him. The Roman Senate had been growing in power for years – largely at the expense of the pope – and now there was a popular movement to restore the old republican traditions, divest the Church of its temporal power, and return the city to its ancient greatness.

The leader of this movement was a monk by the name of Arnold of Brescia, and he so thoroughly whipped up public sentiment that Adrian became a virtual prisoner on the Vatican Hill. Adrian responded by adopting the unprecedented tactic of excommunicating the entire city, essentially declaring war on Rome. No tourists, church services, baptisms, weddings, or burials in consecrated ground would be allowed until the interdict was lifted. It was a daring manoeuvre for a new, foreign pope to attempt given the mood of the day, but the gambit worked. Arnold resisted until the Wednesday of Holy Week, but the prospect of an Easter without the sacrament (much less the lucrative tourist trade) undermined his support. By Thursday morning he had been expelled by his own partisans and Adrian celebrated the Easter mass in triumph.

The victory pacified Rome for the moment, but did little to settle the rest of the North. Barbarossa, meanwhile, was in no mood to deal with republican idealists. When the northern Italian town of Tortona resisted in the name of republicanism, he demolished it stone by stone and deported the entire population. Still in a foul mood, he then turned towards Rome.

Adrian was caught in an uncomfortable position. He was painfully aware of how fragile his grip on Rome was with the populace still dreaming of self-rule, and he mistrusted an over-powerful Barbarossa. Having won a temporary victory against the republicans he had no desire to become a pawn of the German emperor. He set up camp outside of the city and waited.

Their meeting was not a smooth one. The emperor intend-ed to enter Rome as its master, and the pope just as stubbornly insisted on maintaining his dignity. Barbarossa began by quar-reling over protocol. He refused to perform the customary act of guiding the pope's horse on foot, protesting that he was not a groom, but Adrian made it clear that there would be no entry into Rome without it. Barbarossa withdrew in a huff, but when it became clear that the pope wouldn't budge, he had the meet-ing restaged and grudgingly performed the homage.

With that unpleasantness out of the way, the two came to an agreement. Under no circumstances would either make peace with William of Sicily, the emperor Manuel, or the republican commune in Rome. In return Adrian agreed to excommunicate Barbarossa's enemies, while the emperor would enforce the pope's authority.

Adrian had chosen to meet outside of Rome for good

reason. As the two rode in state towards the gates they were met by messengers from the commune who informed the pair that they would only be admitted to the city if Barbarossa first offered a 'gift' of five thousand pounds of gold and guaranteed their ancestral 'rights'. They then launched into a long speech about the glorious heritage of Rome. Barbarossa interrupted mid-sentence with a curt "Rome's greatness is behind it. I have not come to give gifts but to claim what is mine".

With that the two marched into the city, and Barbarossa was crowned. However, the coronation proved to be a bridge too far for the citizens. News of an imperial coronation in a city intoxicated by the thought of independence caused a frenzy, and a mob assaulted the procession as Barbarossa was leaving the cathedral. The emperor was caught unprepared and street fighting raged long into the night. By the next morning order had been restored, but casualties had been terrible on both sides. The German barons had no more stomach for Italy and made it clear that they wished to return home, and Barbarossa, a feudal monarch, was unable to resist them. Adrian begged him to continue with the original plan of invading Sicily, but within a month the Germans were gone.

The pope was now dangerously exposed. He had weakened his own position in Rome for Barbarossa and had received nothing tangible in return. Fortunately, however, there was another emperor at hand. Manuel Comnenus had been preparing his own invasion, and he dispatched a letter to the pope with the extraordinary offer to be the 'sword-arm of the Church'[1]. It didn't matter to Adrian who crushed the Norman kingdom; if the Germans wouldn't help, then the distant Byzantines were an acceptable surrogate. He wrote to Manuel giving him his full blessing for an attack on Sicily.

The Byzantine monarch was a consummate diplomat, and

his agents found ready allies in Italy. The Norman barons of the
peninsula had never really been reconciled to being ruled from
Palermo. More than a decade had passed since Roger II had
reined them in, and the relatively light hand of his successor
was seen as weakness. Byzantine gold encouraged the natural
desire to revolt, and before long an uprising was spreading
throughout the south.

Together, the Norman rebels and the Byzantines posed a
more formidable threat to Sicily than even the Germans had.
The barons provided local knowledge and an army, and Manuel
provided a supply fleet and unlimited funds to raise fresh troops.

To soften up Sicily for an invasion, the rebels turned on any
mainland Italian city that remained loyal to William. The first
target, Bari, was the most important Norman stronghold in
Italy and Manuel was especially eager to recover it. Less than a
century before it had been part of the Byzantine Empire, and
most of the population was still Greek. The royalist defenders
prepared to resist, but when the allied army drew up to the
gates, the locals opened them, resulting in a general massacre
of anyone loyal to Palermo.

The fall of Bari was a major blow to the Norman kingdom,
and it shook the loyalty of the Italian cities that hadn't joined
the rebels. To make matters worse William fell seriously ill, and
in the absence of a response from Palermo, morale on the mainland plummeted. The king's admiral, Maio, eventually sent an
army to aid the beleaguered peninsula, but its general refused to
engage the rebels for several months. When he finally did, the
result was another fiasco. The royal army was wiped out and the
few coastal towns that had wavered moved into the rebel camp.
By the beginning of winter virtually all of Apulia had crumbled.

By now William's rule seemed on the verge of collapse. In
only six short months the emperor Manuel had seemingly

restored Byzantine power in Italy to the level it had been before
the Normans arrived, and he showed no signs of stopping. The
imperial armies were poised to enter Calabria and if that fell –
which it undoubtedly would – the Byzantine force would be
separated from Sicily by a thin stretch of water only a mile wide.

Since the king was ill, the Normans' poor showing was
blamed completely on his powerful minister Maio. Several
plots to assassinate him were launched, but Maio's extensive
network of secret police managed to foil them. When it
became clear that the hated minister couldn't be removed
covertly, a rebellion broke out on the island demanding
his execution.

William had been a laconic ruler, but the direct threat to his
government finally roused him to action. Gathering the royal
army he descended on the rebel camp with surprising speed,
Maio prominently at his side. The rebel leaders were given an
ultimatum: surrender and suffer exile or be killed. A few tried
to protest that they had the king's interests at heart, but Maio
clearly still had William's favor, and an assault on him was an
assault on the king. Faced with such royal determination, the
revolt crumbled and its leaders accepted exile.

Now that he had been shaken out of his lethargy, William's
blood was up. In the spring campaigning season he crossed over
to the mainland with his army and navy. His timing couldn't
have been better. The inspired Byzantine general Michael
Palaeologus, architect of the overall imperial strategy, had just
died, bringing the Byzantine advance to a halt. Now, at the sight
of the entire armed might of Norman Sicily descending on their
camp, the rebels deserted their imperial allies. The Byzantines
didn't stand a chance, and in just over an hour most of them
were dead. Byzantium's gains in the entire war were revealed as
illusory, based on anti-Norman feeling rather than real strength.

Byzantine power in Italy was broken permanently.

William marched unopposed to Bari, determined to punish the city for its massacre of the garrison. The leading citizens met him outside the gates and begged him to show mercy. He granted most of them their lives but razed the city, sparing only the cathedral of St Nicholas and a few other churches.

The rebel barons weren't so lucky. They had by now realized the error of abandoning their Byzantine allies as each had to face the wrath of William on their own. One by one they were captured, tied with weights and thrown into the sea. By the summer it was over. The king's final stop before returning to Palermo was Benevento, where he signed a treaty with the pope recognizing the kingdom of Sicily's right to exist and confirming all of William's claims in Italy.

It had been a remarkably successful campaign, and it had the added benefit of convincing the Byzantine emperor Manuel to make peace. The emperor had come to the conclusion that Barbarossa was a more pressing threat, and that he needed to pit the pope against the German monarch. If Pope Adrian had come to terms with William, then the Byzantines would as well. Manuel initiated peace talks while at the same time cleverly funding a fresh rebellion in Italy to sweeten the eventual deal. William got the point. Convinced that a generous agreement with Byzantium was the only way to avoid perpetual rebellions, he released all Byzantine prisoners and signed a thirty-year peace treaty.

When William returned to Palermo, he again slipped into the pleasurable stupor of palace life. Administrative responsibilities were handed over to Maio, who spent his time strengthening the Sicilian position in Italy to guard against the possibility of Barbarossa's return.

While the king was focused on frivolity, and his chief

minister concentrated on the mainland, the rest of the empire started to decay. In 1155 a Muslim revolt started in North Africa, and the badly outnumbered Normans were unable to suppress it. Urgent requests to Palermo for aid were ignored and by 1159 all of Tripoli except the trading city of Mahdia had fallen. William sent a small fleet to aid the city, but it was destroyed by a storm and he didn't bother himself further.

The Normans in Mahdia bravely held out for over a year waiting vainly for the expected relieving army. Finally they struck a deal; they would send a delegation to Palermo and if it returned empty handed they would voluntarily surrender. A small group set out, but when they reached the capital they were bluntly told by Maio that the city wasn't worth the expense it would take to preserve it. The stunned ambassadors returned, Mahdia surrendered, and the Norman empire in Africa ceased to exist.

Maio may have been correct in his assessment of the situation; certainly his efforts in Italy were paying off. With Sicilian backing, the northern Italian cities had formed the great Lombard league and successfully held off a German invasion. After several years spent fruitlessly trying to cow the peninsula into submission, even the iron-willed Barbarossa was forced to admit that Italy was outside of his grasp.

For all the international success of Maio's policies, however, he remained deeply unpopular in Sicily. To the local Sicilians he represented the worst type of autocrat. Over-powerful, arrogant, and unresponsive to public moods, he had sat by and watched while North Africa burned, and his coreligionists suffered. Even worse, as far as the local nobility were concerned, was Maio's habit of elevating Greeks or Arabs to positions of power over the heads of established aristocratic Normans. The fact that these appointees were qualified, capable individuals, or that the Sicilian Normans were all too often entitled, incompetent, and boorish, was irrelevant. Maio, a foreigner himself from Bari, was the fountainhead of everything that ailed Sicily.

In the autumn of 1160 the admiral got word that his prospective son-in-law was implicated in the latest attempt to kill him. For all his savvy, he succumbed to the conceit that someone so close couldn't be involved, and a week later he was struck down in the streets of Palermo. The news electrified the city, and the assassin, a man named Matthew Bonnellus became an instant celebrity. Fearing reprisals from the king for killing his favorite, Bonnellus fled and serious rioting instantly broke out.

With half of Palermo in flames, William finally stirred. The mob was suppressed with difficulty, and for the first time the king fully realized how hated Maio had been. Facing a wave of popular unrest, he was forced to pardon everyone involved in the murder of his most trusted lieutenant, even gallingly awarding Bonnellus the title 'savior of the kingdom' for his part in the brutal deed.

His new status as beloved icon went straight to Bonnellus' head. Stepping into Maio's position wasn't enough: he now schemed to get rid of William as well. While Bonnellus absented himself from Palermo to avoid the taint of regicide, a group of dissatisfied nobles had William seized in one of his palaces. The king desperately tried to jump out of a window to avoid his captors, but he was restrained, and the entire royal family was arrested. If they had appointed a new king at that moment, William's reign would have been finished, but the conspirators couldn't decide whether to kill William or simply have him abdicate in favor of his nine-year-old son Roger. While they argued about who would receive the crown, their followers began to systematically loot the main palace.

As they squabbled, the mood in the city started to harden against them. William's reign may have had its share of disasters, but he wasn't directly blamed, only the men around him acting in his name. It was one thing to get rid of a hated minister, and quite another to so mistreat an anointed king. The looting of the palace and the arrest of the royal family was enough to convince the citizens of Palermo who the real villains were. The palace was stormed again, and the terrified rebels ran to the captive William and begged him to save them.

William complied and the rebels were allowed to leave, but the ordeal broke him. During the fighting his eldest son and heir had been killed, and when the first of his guards reached him they found him huddled in a corner sobbing.

The rest of his reign passed in peace. In his last decade he left the capital of Palermo only once for a triumphal procession through Italy to install his candidate for pope in Rome[2]. Most of William's time was spent in pleasurable pursuits, particularly the construction of a lavish new palace complex with fishponds, fountains, pools, and well-stocked hunting grounds. In the spring of 1166 he contracted a fever and, after a two-month illness, he died.

History has not been kind to William. His main chronicler despised him, and is responsible for his epithet, 'the Bad'. The king's excessive lifestyle was the root of much of this displeasure. If his father was the baptized sultan, it was snidely put, William hardly bothered with the baptism.

In 1166, however, William was genuinely mourned. Palermo hung itself with black for three days, and the king's body was taken reverently to the cathedral where it was placed in a simple porphyry sarcophagus. His oldest surviving son, a thirteen-year-old boy also named William, was crowned, and all of Sicily seemed to be at peace.

He was not a great king, nor perhaps even a good one. The many rebellions, the loss of North Africa, and the general shirking of his responsibility as king, all rightfully stained his reputation. But he also had the impossible task of following a legendary father without the benefit of guidance or preparation. In the circumstances, his defense of Norman Sicily against a determined pope and two of the greatest emperors to ever sit on their respective thrones was a remarkable feat. It was a fleeting glimpse of what could have been.

Chapter Fifteen

WILLIAM THE WORSE

William I may have acquired the nickname 'bad', but at least he provided the kingdom with an heir. The great vitality of the Normans in southern Italy had been failing for some time. William's father and grandfather had fathered at least thirty-two children between them while William managed only four, but at least the succession wasn't in doubt. The young William II, just shy of his thirteenth birthday, was crowned in a sumptuous ceremony, and theoretically accepted the burden of caring for nearly two million subjects. He was by all accounts a striking youth. Tall and dark-eyed, already showing the fair hair and height of his Norse heritage, he seemed a mixture of dynamism and gravity far beyond his years. According to several eye-witnesses, at the first glimpse of him in the streets of Palermo his subjects fell genuinely in love.

Until he came of age, however, they would be denied the pleasure of being governed by him. In the meantime a Regency Council was set up headed by his mother Margaret and a trio of the leading notables of the kingdom. It would have been difficult to pick a more unsuitable group of people to run a government. The three advisors – a eunuch named Peter, a notary named Matthew, and the English archbishop Richard Palmer – spent most of their time trying to assassinate each

other. Margaret soon realized that she had to get rid of them
before they got rid of her, so she promoted the least threatening
one – Peter – above the other two, momentarily putting one
of the most wealthy and influential Christian kingdoms in the
hands of a Muslim eunuch.

Peter was an intriguer, a civil servant who knew the
intricacies of the bureaucracy, and who was most comfortable
behind the scenes. Pushed to the center, he quickly lost
control. Within a few months Sicily was in chaos, and fearing
assassination, Peter fled to North Africa. To restore the
situation, Margaret invited her cousin Stephen du Perche from
France, who, if not wise, was at least strong.

The choice was instantly controversial. It was bad enough
that the best jobs were being awarded to foreigners, but the
salary of the office of chancellor, vacant since Peter had
fled, had been divided among the nobility who now angrily
resented Margaret. Stephen's appointment was a loss of both
prestige and income.

Just as tensions reached a boiling pitch, however, news came
of a fresh disaster that made everything else irrelevant. The terrible German emperor Barbarossa had crossed the Alps and descended on Italy. The very survival of the kingdom was in doubt.

Sicily had been a thorn in the German side since its
founding. Norman kings had offered aid and protection to the
pope and the cities of northern Italy, which had time and again
defied the emperor. Army after army had been sent to pacify
Italy, only to have it flare up again in revolt the moment they
left, aided by Sicilian gold and papal blessing. The solution,
obviously, in Barbarossa's eyes was twofold. Install a tame
pontiff in Rome, and smash Sicily.

There were many in Palermo who blamed their late king for
the bad news. Barbarossa had started out the following spring

and had made it explicitly clear that he was coming to stop William the Bad's meddling and shatter the Norman kingdom once and for all. The fact that William had died in the meantime, and that his successor was a mere boy, was irrelevant.

What had finally goaded the German monarch to action was the part the late William had played in one of the most bizarre elections in papal history seven years prior, exacerbating the rift between Aachen and Palermo. When a papal vacancy had appeared, Frederick made it clear that he supported a pliable cardinal by the name of Octavian. The assembled clergy, however, tired of imperial interference and confident of Norman support, voted unanimously for a man named Alexander. This should have settled the matter, but Octavian, thoroughly convinced that he should have been pope, wasn't about to let an election stand in his way. On coronation day, when pope-elect Alexander bowed his head to receive the mantle, Octavian leapt forward and wrenched it from the hands of the startled cardinals. In the uproar that followed, the flailing Octavian lost control of the garment. He then produced an identical one brought for just such a turn of events, and managed to get it on backwards before bolting to the papal throne with the howling clerics at his heels.

Octavian reached the throne just before his pursuers, managing to declare himself Pope Victor IV. With the timely arrival of some hired thugs, the newly-minted pope ordered everyone to acclaim him. His rival, the Norman-supported pope Alexander, was taken to a nearby fortress and imprisoned, and Octavian settled back to enjoy his tenure.

Despite hefty bribes by the imperial ambassadors, Octavian's reputation plummeted as news of his shocking behavior spread throughout Rome. Appearances in public were greeted with catcalls or worse, and mobs gathered outside of his palace to taunt him. After two weeks of abuse he could take no more and slipped out of Rome.

Barbarossa's failure to impose his pope on Rome was galling enough, but his creature's behaviour after being evicted had made things worse. Denied Rome, Octavian had settled in the hills surrounding the city of Lucca, and there the self-proclaimed spiritual head of Christendom became a bandit, waylaying pilgrims traveling through Tuscany.

A bit of tact from Sicily might still have prevented a war with the humiliated German monarch, but William the Bad chose instead to send an honour guard to escort the Norman-supported Alexander back to Rome, publicly broadcasting the fact that Frederick was powerless to enforce his will in Italy. William the Bad had then, with his usual timing, expired, leaving his successors to deal with the consequences of offending Barbarossa.

A combined Norman and Italian army was sent to slow the German advance, but this only enraged the emperor further. After annihilating this meager force, Barbarossa razed several towns, driving their populations into the surrounding countryside. The road to Rome was choked with refugees, all hoping that the magic of its name would somehow ward off the invaders. Its fate, however, was sealed. On July 29, 1167 the imperial forces battered their way into Rome, giving full vent to their pent-up emotions. Statues were pulled down, marble slabs were hacked from their fittings, and tombs were smashed open to get at the jewels inside. Not even the basilica of Saint Peter's was spared. Bands of soldiers managed to force their way past the doors and slaughtered the horrified clerics as they clung vainly to the high altar.

The very next day, before the stench of blood and corpses was cleared, Barbarossa had yet another tame antipope crowned, grimly promising that all who resisted him would experience the same fate. In Palermo his words reduced the city to panic. The defense was virtually abandoned, as nobles began to flee with what treasure they could carry. Sicily appeared doomed. It was in chaos, governed by an unpopular woman and an inexperienced foreigner. There wasn't even a real army assembled to oppose the Germans. Only an Act of God could save the Normans now.

Fortunately for Sicily, God obliged. Two days after Barbarossa crowned his pope, the plague struck the imperial army, devastating it. The swampy climate of Rome and the unseasonable heat only made it worse, but when Barbarossa ordered an evacuation of the city the plague followed him. By the time he reached the Alps his great army was ruined. The emperor was no longer feared, but actively mocked. Northern Italy didn't even bother to wait until he was gone to formally declare its independence, and, as if that weren't enough, they blocked all of the passes through the mountains. Only by dressing as a servant did the humiliated emperor manage to sneak past into Germany.

In Sicily, news of the miraculous delivery led to a surge in popularity for Margaret and Stephen du Perche. The French escort that Stephen had brought continued to be resented by the population, but Stephen himself was proving to be a competent administrator. His reforms, however, mostly at the expense of the nobility, were intensely hated by the latter and led to numerous assassination plots. For her part, Margaret supported him completely, and it became clear that none of the nobility would ever share power while he was present. For two years things continued relatively smoothly, with Stephen nimbly evading assassination and managing the growing resentment of the population.

All would have been well if Margaret had maintained the status quo, but she antagonized the populace by appointing Stephen archbishop of Palermo. A mob stormed the palace, forcing Stephen and his French companions to flee to the cathedral and barricade themselves inside. Bloodshed was avoided only when Stephen agreed to leave Sicily and never return. He and his companions were allowed to walk down to the harbor and board a ship destined for the Holy Land.

The fall of her favorite finished Margaret. Although William still had three years before he reached his majority, 'that Spanish woman', as she was called, had no energy to continue. She remained the regent, but real power devolved to her son's tutor, an ambitious and unscrupulous Englishman by the name of Walter of the Mill. Raised to the rank of archbishop, Walter would have a virtual monopoly of power over domestic affairs for the next decade.

In 1171, William turned eighteen, and officially took control over Sicily. Although he had lived his life in seclusion in the palace, he already had grandiose ambitions. Sicily had once been the leading power in the Mediterranean and William intended to return it to that state. To his subjects at least, he seemed uniquely suited to the task. Tall and good looking, with a round face, dark eyes, and a closely cropped beard, he was studious, fluent in at least five languages, and deeply religious. He was also remarkably fortunate. The upheaval of Stephen du Perche's fall turned out to be the last serious disturbance of his reign. Sicily entered a remarkable period of domestic peace and prosperity.

The kingdom's trade boomed. The secret of silk production was smuggled out of Constantinople, adding to the already diverse industries of iron, salt, and sulfur. Coral was harvested from the coastal waters, the Sicilian tunny fish was imported across the Mediterranean, and Sicilian farms produced wheat, oranges, lemons, melons, and almonds that were in demand across Europe and North Africa. Even Sicily's forests played their part. Sicilian timber was well enough known for its quality that at least one pope used it exclusively to repair the Lateran's roof.

The turmoil of William the Bad's reign had interfered with these industries, but it hadn't affected Sicily's reputation for luxury or power. When the young William II attained his majority, foreign offers of marriage rolled in. The first was from the Byzantine emperor Manuel Comnenus, offering his fifteen-year-old daughter Maria. This was especially intriguing because Manuel didn't have a son, meaning that William's grandchild would stand to inherit both Sicily and the Byzantine Empire. Not to be outdone, Frederick Barbarossa offered his daughter as well, and Henry II of England chimed in with the offer of his third daughter Joan, sister of Richard the Lionheart.

With the Englishman, Walter of the Mill, advising him, William gravitated towards Joan. It was only natural, after all, that the two Norman kingdoms at opposite ends of Europe should be officially united. There were already cultural and family ties; each kingdom was a natural destination for the exiles of the other, and most of the nobility in Palermo had relatives in London.

Just when William was on the point of accepting, however, the Archbishop of Canterbury, Thomas à Becket, was murdered by four of Henry's knights, and in the resulting firestorm the matter was tactfully dropped. The emperor Manuel again offered his daughter and this time it was accepted. On the day when the princess was due to arrive, however, there was no Byzantine ship on the horizon. Manuel had evidently decided that the Western Empire would be a more suitable match, and didn't bother to inform Sicily of the change of plan. William processed down to the harbor in a state and after a day of waiting was forced to return to the palace thoroughly – and quite publicly – humiliated. He wouldn't forget the insult.

For several years the marriage issue was allowed to lie fallow before Walter of the Mill again began to suggest that William should look towards England. He received surprising help in this direction from the pope who was terrified that William would marry into Barbarossa's family and thereby unite the two great powers to the north and south of Rome. Enough time had passed for most of the furor over Becket's murder to die down, and inquiries were quietly made. Henry and his wife Eleanor of Aquitaine accepted, and in 1177 the twenty-three-year-old William and the twelve-year-old Joan were married in Palermo.

Politically, the match marked the highpoint of William's reign. He was at the peak of his youth, beginning even to break free from the control of Walter of the Mill. Three years before he had started building a magnificent cathedral at Monreale, ostensibly to the glory of his grandfather Roger II, but in reality to weaken Walter's power. When it was finished he appointed an archbishop, creating at once a rival of equal authority to his powerful advisor. Walter protested furiously, but there was little he could do.

It was an extraordinary time. William was popular, fabulously wealthy, and young, and the international situation seemed to adjust itself for his benefit. In Italy the aging Frederick Barbarossa at last abandoned any hopes of outright conquest and decided to try diplomacy instead. He offered Sicily a permanent truce. It was too late for William to marry into the German royal family, but Frederick had another offer. His son and heir Henry was not yet married; if William could find a suitable bride, the two kingdoms would be united in peace.

William eagerly agreed. His grandfather Roger II had a posthumous daughter named Constance who was a year younger than William himself. Since he didn't yet have any children, his aunt Constance stood to inherit the Sicilian throne. This point was driven home by having all the nobles of the realm swear to accept her as his heir if he died without issue. He then escorted her to the harbor and sent her off to the crown prince of the German Empire.

Even some of William's usually adoring public recognized the sheer lunacy of what he had just done. Although there seemed to be plenty of time for heirs – he was just thirty and his wife was eighteen – it was a terrible risk to give Sicily's great enemy a legitimate claim to the throne. If William or his wife were to die prematurely – and the medieval world was nothing if not uncertain – Sicily would fall into the lap of the ruler who had actively tried to destroy it for the last quarter of a century.

For William it was worth the risk, simply because it freed him up to concentrate on his dream of foreign conquest. He had grown up on stories of his grandfather's triumphs, and had been appalled by his father's abandonment of Africa. Now he intended to revive Sicily's overseas empire.

His first probing attack was a disaster. North Africa was united under the powerful Almohads, and they easily repulsed the Norman invasion. Next, he sent thirty thousand troops to invade Alexandria, hoping to curb the power of the new Muslim strongman, Saladin, who was threatening Jerusalem. The Normans had barely disembarked when Saladin's army showed up, easily routing the disorganized Sicilians. Most reached the ships in safety, but they had to retreat with nothing accomplished. William, however, was nothing if not determined, and the situation in the eastern Mediterranean was suddenly very encouraging in the most surprising of places – Constantinople.

1180 saw a great changing of the guard across the Mediterranean world. Manuel Comnenus died after thirty-six years on the throne, leaving an eleven-year-old named Alexius and a deeply unpopular regent. For two years the government held on, but in 1182 Manuel's cousin, Andronicus, raised a revolt.

Andronicus was a curious figure, possessing all of the brilliance of his family with none of its restraint. In 1182 he was already in his sixties but looked two decades younger, and his exploits, both on the battlefield and in the bedroom, were legendary. By the time he marched on Constantinople he had already seduced three cousins, been banished twice, and had acquired a reputation as an innovative – if slightly eccentric – general. His effect on the population was magnetic. Wherever he went he was greeted with open arms. Armies sent against him defected, and when he arrived at the walls of Constantinople, he was escorted through the Golden Gate by ecstatic crowds.

The cheering didn't last long. Within a month he had murdered the entire royal family. The young emperor Alexius was made to sign his own mother's death warrant before being strangled himself. Andronicus then married the twelve-year-old widow and started to systematically eliminate anyone who showed sympathy for the previous regime.

In Sicily, William saw a chance to avenge the public humiliation he had suffered at Constantinople's hands. Affairs at home were carefully put in order. A treaty with North Africa ensured that there would be no threat from that quarter, and the German Empire had already been neutralized by the marriage to Constance. A Sicilian Greek was found and put forward as the murdered Alexius II, and William piously announced that he would restore the youth to his rightful throne. The largest force the kingdom had ever mustered was prepared, and in the spring of 1185 two hundred and fifty ships carrying eighty thousand men set sail from Palermo.

They reached the port city of Durrës on the Dalmatian coast in June, and thirteen days later it was in their hands. They now had access to the Via Egnatia, the old Roman road that ran across the Balkans to the city of Thessalonica and then to Constantinople itself.

Thanks to an effective news blockade before they set out, the Norman army had managed to take Durrës by surprise, but Thessalonica promised to be a much more formidable obstacle. It was the second largest city of the Byzantine Empire, and its military governor had over a month's warning to prepare his defenses.

Fortunately for the Normans he failed to make even rudimentary plans beyond shutting the doors. Within a few days his archers had run out of arrows and his catapults had run out of stones. Even worse, he hadn't bothered to check the water supply and several of the half-filled cisterns were found to be leaking badly. Instead of trying to address the situation he decided to profit from it, rationing off his personal supply for enormous sums. Morale plummeted steadily and it wasn't long before a desperate defender opened a gate.

The destruction was terrible. The Normans entered in the early morning and by noon more than five thousand citizens were dead. By the end of the first day, the generals had managed to reassert control of the situation, but Thessalonica was in ruins. The Norman army in any case had to keep moving. Food and water were by now scarce, and even at the best of times no city was capable of handling an influx of eighty thousand new people. The Sicilians left a small garrison behind and quickly resumed their march towards Constantinople. With any luck they would be eating Christmas dinner in the imperial palace.

The Byzantines didn't seem capable of stopping them. Andronicus was showing signs of mental instability, and his reign was descending into a bloodbath. As one chronicler put it, 'he considered a day without killing someone as a day wasted'. One moment he would show remorse, seemingly tormented by the blood on his hands, and the next he would be rising to new extremes of killing. Terrified of assassination, he barricaded himself inside the palace, spending his time rooting out real or imagined conspiracies. When news of the Norman army reached him, he dispatched a force to intercept it, but since he was incapable of trusting anyone, he split it into five parts, each commanded by a minor general of equal rank. They immediately started quarreling about the best course of action, some wandering in the general direction of the Sicilians, and others taking defensive positions along the way.

When the citizens of Constantinople woke a few weeks later to see the Norman fleet drawn up in the imperial harbor, a mob stormed the palace, and Andronicus the Terrible met a grisly end. With his fall, the empire's luck abruptly changed. The new emperor Isaac II consolidated the splintered imperial army under its most gifted general Alexius Branas and he immediately marched two hundred miles to confront the Normans. William's overconfident army had dropped its guard, and Branas successfully ambushed it as the Sicilians were attempting to cross a river.

The casualties were relatively light, but the effect on morale was devastating. The Normans had expected an easy victory, but it was clear that the approach to Constantinople, to say nothing of the eventual siege that would be needed, was going to be long and difficult. Branas cleverly waited a few months for morale to dip further before offering to discuss terms. When the Sicilians hesitated, Branas suddenly attacked. The Normans were taken off guard, and since their fleet was in Constantinople, there was nowhere to run. Much of the army was destroyed. Those that survived tried to take refuge in Thessalonica, but were gleefully attacked by the citizens as payback for the sacking of the city. Only a few thousand of the grand army managed to hike over the mountain passes in winter and return to Italy.

The debacle was a serious blow to William's prestige, but the silver lining was that his navy was still undefeated; they had easily conquered several islands and had brushed aside the Byzantine fleet. The campaign had even revealed an admiral of genius named Margaritus. In 1187 the entire Christian world had need of his services.

In the late fall of that year, a Genoese trading vessel sailed up the Tiber and put in at the port of Trastevere. Not bothering to wait for a formal invitation, the two ambassadors it carried hurried straight to the Lateran Palace and demanded an interview with Pope Urban III. They brought word that the unthinkable had happened. Jerusalem had fallen to the Saracens and the True Cross – Christendom's holiest relic – had been captured. It was too much for the aged pontiff to bear. Urban withdrew to his private quarters in shock and died a few days later.

It didn't take long for the horrified West to react. The day after Urban III was buried, his successor issued a papal bull calling for a crusade. When the dispatch reached Sicily it found the Norman kingdom already in motion. Word of the terrible events had already arrived in Palermo, and William II had lost no time in his preparations. Dressing in a rough shirt of camel hair and smearing ashes over his head, he ordered four days of mourning and pledged his immediate support for the crusade. It would take time to gather his army, but as a sign of his intentions he dispatched his gifted admiral, Margaritus, to Palestine with orders to harass the Saracens.

The pope would have been hard pressed to find a more ideal spokesman for the crusade. Mild-mannered and deeply religious, William was immensely popular at home, and well-connected abroad. Like his father and grandfather before him, he was fluent in all three major languages of his kingdom, and was willing to accommodate his Muslim, Orthodox, and Jewish subjects. As befitted the main actor of a great movement, he was famous for his beauty – more than one observer had compared him to an angel at his coronation – and now in his early thirties he clearly showed his Hauteville blood, towering over his contemporaries. Perhaps most important from the pope's perspective, however, was the fact that he had fully inherited his family's taste for battle. If he had yet to display its corresponding traits of charisma or strategic sense, it was only because he was still young and relatively untested. Such concerns in any case could be left to subordinates; the king's main function would be as a dashing figurehead.

In this respect at least he performed magnificently. Firing off letters to Henry II of England, Philip Augustus of France, and Frederick Barbarossa of Germany, he managed to convince all of them to personally lead armies to recapture Jerusalem. There was more than simple Christian piety driving William to take pen in hand, however. If the Crusaders could be diverted through Sicily it would be a huge financial windfall for his merchants. Each letter contained not only an appeal to religious duty but also a nice bit of propaganda stressing the pleasant Sicilian climate and highlighting the numerous advantages of a sea-route to Palestine.

These appeals were bolstered by the brilliant performance of William's admiral in the Holy Land. With a tiny fleet of sixty ships, Margaritus was managing to keep the main Crusader sea-lanes open, building up a steady pressure on the coast, and thwarting every Saracen attempt to capture a Latin port. By the summer of 1188 he was being called the 'new Neptune' and was justly feared throughout the eastern Mediterranean. News of his approach off the coast of Tripoli forced the Muslims to raise the siege of the nearby Krak des Chevaliers[1], and his appearance in Tyre the next year caused an immediate Saracen retreat. The only thing preventing him from capturing new territory was a lack of knights – he had less than two hundred with him – but the arrival of the main Crusading armies would change that. Then in mid-November came terrible news that threw everything into chaos. William II, last of the Hauteville kings, was dead.

The cause of his death is unknown. It was only reported to have been swift and relatively peaceful. His reign was remembered as a golden age of internal peace and prosperity, and he was mourned more than any king in Sicily before or after. Several centuries later Dante even put him in paradise as the ideal king. This reputation, however, is thoroughly undeserved. William II was less 'good' than he was fortunate; his reign was bookmarked by periods of severe instability that made his own rule seem ideal by comparison. There were incessant revolts during his father's reign and civil war after his death. If there was peace and prosperity in between it was not due to any wise stewardship on his part. He was remarkably irresponsible. Not only did he constantly commit Sicily's resources to ill-advised and uniformly disastrous foreign wars, but he also signed away his kingdom's future to its greatest enemy for the short-term gain of a temporary peace. His predecessors, even William the Bad, had defended Sicily against the German Empire with everything they had, and he gave it away of his own free will. Then, like all irresponsible leaders, he left his successors to pay the price.

Chapter Sixteen

THE MONKEY KING

William II's great failure – uncharacteristically for a Hauteville – was that he didn't produce a son. When he died suddenly at age thirty-six the kingdom was thrown into a succession crisis. Thankfully, the absence of a king didn't initially disrupt day-to-day affairs since Roger II's magnificent civil service kept things temporarily running. No state, however, could afford to be headless for too long, and while there was no shortage of ambitious pretenders, there were only three serious claimants. The official heir was the late king's aunt, Constance. A few objected because of her gender, but what made her unsuitable to most Sicilians was the fact that she was currently married to Henry VI, crown prince of Sicily's mortal enemy, the German Empire.

The opposition party crystallized around two noblemen, Tancred of Lecce and Roger of Andria. On the surface they seemed evenly matched. Both were decorated war heroes with plenty of titles and awards, and could boast long careers of service to the state. Roger drew support from the nobility while Tancred was popular with the minor barons and the masses. The real distinguishing feature, however, was one of blood. Roger could only muster a distant link to the throne; he was a great-grandson of Drogo de Hauteville, while Tancred was the illegitimate grandson of Roger II. Proximity to the loved Roger – no matter how tenuous the legitimacy – was a stronger claim. The pope, desperate to prevent a German take-over of Sicily, threw his support behind Tancred, and in January of 1190 he was crowned king of Sicily.

The new king was short, swarthy, and unusually ugly. A contemporary historian nicknamed him 'Tancredulous' and snidely remarked that he resembled a monkey. "Behold," he wrote at Tancred's coronation, "an ape is crowned!" If physically lacking, however, Tancred was also energetic, smart, and ambitious. He had been involved in the coup of 1161, personally storming the palace and taking William the Bad prisoner. When the rebellion collapsed he had accepted exile in exchange for official pardon and, given the king's less than sterling reputation, emerged from the whole ordeal with his name unscathed.

He had need of every bit of his political skills almost immediately. At the news of his coronation the kingdom's long-simmering religious tensions boiled over. The Muslim population had been declining since the Normans had first conquered Sicily. Under Roger II they had been an influential and respected minority, but with each year they had been steadily disenfranchised with the influx of Italians from the mainland. After William II had died, they threw their support behind Constance, figuring that the foreign Germans would be glad of allies, and Tancred's success was therefore a crushing blow. When a group of Christians unwisely assaulted a mosque in Palermo, the entire Muslim population of Sicily erupted.

Tancred sent soldiers to stabilize the situation, and the Arabs fled to the surrounding hills where they seized several castles. Somehow Tancred managed to confine the rebellion to the western part of the island, but it took the better part of a year to suppress it.

Part of the reason that it smoldered on for so long was that Tancred was distracted with ominous news from northern Europe. The German emperor, Frederick Barbarossa, had drowned while on crusade, leaving the empire to his energetic son. Henry VI had been an intimidating enemy when he was merely a prince, and now he was an emperor. As the Muslim revolt blazed in Sicily, Henry crossed the Alps and invaded Italy. He had two aims. The first was to claim the Iron Crown of Lombardy, a golden diadem that had once belonged to the Roman emperor Constantine and was called 'iron' because it supposedly contained a nail from Christ's Crucifixion[1]. The second was to install himself, with his wife Constance at his side of course, on the throne of Sicily.

Lombardy posed no obstacle. When Henry appeared in Rome with his army in 1191, the frightened pope crowned him master of northern Italy and the Western Empire. Henry's second objective also looked within easy reach. News of his approach had the usual effect, throwing the south into chaos. Besides the familiar rebellious barons, there were now a growing number of Normans in the kingdom who supported Henry's invasion. Most of them were fatalists who believed that the smart play was to get in the emperor's good graces, but some had also made the calculation that a distant ruler in Germany would be less intrusive than a local king in Palermo. When Henry entered Norman territory in the spring, he found virtually the entire southern part of the peninsula in open revolt.

Tancred couldn't leave Sicily to restore the situation because he was too pressed with the Muslim revolt and was still consolidating his power. Nevertheless, he acted quickly. A large amount of gold was sent to his general on the mainland to raise troops and bribe towns to stay loyal. This decisiveness – and a stroke of luck – saved Tancred. The summer heat, always Sicily's greatest defender, took its toll on the Germans, and when Tancred's army sharply defeated their advance force, Henry decided to withdraw. Without imperial support, the rebellion collapsed as well. Their ringleader, the same Roger of Andria that had earlier contested the throne, was captured and executed.

Tancred's nerve had saved the situation, but he understood that he had merely won a short reprieve from Henry's invasion. He didn't have long to savor the victory. Richard the Lionheart, king of Norman England, was heading for Sicily.

Although he had been on the throne only a year longer than Tancred, Richard's reputation as a heroic adventurer was already well known. He had been commanding armies in the field since he was sixteen, more than half his life by 1191, and was widely viewed as the one figure who could rescue Jerusalem from the Saracens. The Holy City had fallen three years before in 1188 triggering a call for a new crusade, and the kings of Europe had immediately pledged their support. Richard, to the pope's delight, had agreed to lead it on the condition that Philip Augustus, the king of France, would go with him. This wasn't done out of a sense of royal fraternity but because Richard didn't trust his colleague and rightly suspected that Philip would confiscate his French lands the moment he was out of the country. William the Good, seeing a potential windfall from the increased trade that would follow in the crusade's wake, had written to the pair before his death, suggesting that Sicily would make an ideal launching point. They had both agreed and it now fell to Tancred to play reluctant host.

King Richard was a difficult guest at the best of times. Despite his reputation as the pinnacle of chivalry, he was easily bored and far more interested in adventuring than ruling. During his ten-year reign he spent barely six months in England. As the historian Sir Steven Runciman put it, "he was a bad son, a bad husband, and a bad king, but a gallant and splendid soldier". He was also temperamental, and by the time he reached Sicily he was in a foul mood.

There were several causes. He had a tendency to get seasick, and the crossing from Italy had been an unpleasant one. Then, when he arrived in Messina he discovered that Philip had beaten him there and in typical fashion had helped himself to the palace, leaving more modest accommodations for Richard. These annoyances would have been enough to sour his temper, but they were accompanied by a more serious diplomatic problem.

William the Good had, in typical fashion, promised lavish gifts to induce Richard to Sicily and Tancred, who had spent a fortune defending Italy, was refusing to provide them. Even more seriously, however, was Tancred's treatment of William's widow Joanna. She believed that Constance was the rightful sovereign and had somewhat foolishly vocally supported the Germans against Tancred. In response, Tancred had put her under house arrest and confiscated her vast estates. If Joanna had been a minor noble that would have been the end of the matter, but she happened to be Richard's sister.

When Tancred's envoys came to welcome the English king to Sicily, therefore, Richard demanded both Joanna and her entire dowry, and threatened not to leave until he was satisfied. Tancred gave in immediately. He had more than enough on his plate without risking a conflict with a crusading army. Joanna was brought to Richard's residence carrying every cent of her dowry, with a bit extra thrown in as a mark of Tancred's esteem. This should have satisfied Richard's pride, but he was enjoying the Sicilian climate and decided that it would make a splendid base. He raided Calabria, seizing the small town of

San Salvatore to settle Joanna in style, and then returned to Messina and evicted the Greek monks of its finest monastery to garrison his soldiers.

The largely Greek citizens of Messina were horrified. They had welcomed the famous Lionheart with open arms, provided him with entertainment and living quarters, and he had repaid them with hostility and cruelty. The sight of the monks being forcibly removed was the last straw. The populace took to the streets, bringing whatever crude weapons they could find, and rushed Richard's villa.

The English counterattack was merciless. Richard ordered his men to burn any Sicilian ships in the harbor so the mob had nowhere to flee, and then told them to destroy the city. The only thing spared was the great palace at the center where an alarmed Philip Augustus was staying. When it was over, Richard rounded up the survivors and forced them to construct a massive wooden fortress. Just to make sure everyone got the point he named it 'Matagrifon' – 'the Greek Killer'.

Such atrocious behavior rallied all of Sicily around Tancred, but surprisingly he didn't even send a formal protest. He was playing a larger game. No matter how irritating Richard's behavior was, he wasn't a long-term threat. Tancred's real enemy was Henry VI, and he needed any ally that he could find. If he was forced to swallow his pride in his own kingdom to secure Richard's friendship, then that was an acceptable price. So instead of soldiers, Tancred sent a vast sum of gold, enough to allow Richard to travel to the Holy Land in style, and implored him to winter in Sicily.

Richard was enjoying himself, but tensions with the French king were nearly at the breaking point, and there was still the matter of his crusading vow. He therefore refused to stay, but in exchange for another round of gifts, he agreed to recognize Tancred as the rightful king. After Christmas the two met in Palermo and sealed their alliance with a marriage contract between Richard's four-year-old son and Tancred's teenaged daughter. As a sign of his new friendship Richard presented his brother-king with a sword that he claimed was Excalibur[2].

Tancred's patience had paid off, and with the news that Henry was again on the march it seemed just in time. He again begged Richard to stay, but the English king had made up his mind. By April both he and Philip were gone, leaving Sicily alone to deal with the German Empire.

Henry VI was taking his time. He had brought with him his wife, Constance, and the bulk of his army, and knew exactly how weak Tancred's support was on the mainland. When he crossed into the Sicilian kingdom's territory in southern Italy, there was no resistance. Aversa, the first territory the Normans had conquered in Italy, surrendered without a struggle, as did the entire northern part of the kingdom.

Tancred was disappointed, but he probably wasn't surprised. He had concentrated his defenses on the south, and opted to make his stand in Naples. While Tancred's admiral Margaritus kept the port open, the citizens of Naples put up a heroic defense. Even Henry was impressed. He couldn't effectively cut off the city from the sea, which made his siege pointless. With the summer heat making everyone miserable, he decided to withdraw to regroup. As a sign to the Normans that he fully intended to return he left his queen, Constance, with a full garrison at Salerno.

As an act of bravado, it was an impressive show, but it was also a foolish mistake. Henry had badly misjudged the people of southern Italy. The towns and cities that had so quickly joined him were now desperate to prove their loyalty to Sicily.

The citizens of Salerno wasted no time massacring the imperial garrison, and delivered Constance to Palermo.

Norman Sicily had been improbably saved. Without Constance, Henry didn't have the slightest claim to Sicily's throne, and the price of her release would be the recognition of Tancred's kingship. All that was left was for Henry to realize he was beaten, and the long war would be over.

The pope, who was equally pleased that his all-powerful northern neighbor had been checked, wrote to Tancred immediately, offering his endorsement. His letter, however, also contained a devastating request. Amicable relations, it said, could never be achieved if one party held the other's wife prisoner. Tancred was instructed to send Constance to Rome, and the pope would act as arbiter.

Tancred was now caught. If he kept Constance in Palermo he would antagonize his new ally and allow Henry to pose as a righteous crusader against the enemy of the Church. If, on the other hand, he let her out of his control, his one bargaining chip was lost. After a week of agonizing he reluctantly allowed her to cross the straits of Messina that separated Sicily from the mainland and begin the journey to Rome. It took less than a month for his worst fears to be realized. A party of imperial knights ambushed the Normans as they crossed out of Sicilian territory and freed Constance. Within two weeks she was back with Henry and he was making preparations to restore her to her throne.

The silver lining in this disaster was that the pope was now actively campaigning for Tancred. He managed to keep Henry busy by endorsing several rebel German barons, and it took more than nine months for the emperor to finally crush them.

Tancred used the breathing room to search for other allies. Richard the Lionheart was of no use. After the limited success of the Third Crusade, he had been captured by Henry trying to return to England and was now help prisoner at the German court. Richard's brother, John, was in no great hurry to ransom him, but did send several shipments of silver which Henry was busy using to buy and equip a fleet to invade Sicily. Tancred had few other options but to reach out to Byzantium, the one power that was naturally hostile to the German Empire. After some hurried negotiations Tancred convinced the emperor, Isaac II, to agree to a marriage alliance. Unfortunately for Norman Sicily, however, the Byzantines were not in a position to help. Isaac was a weak emperor of a weak dynasty and the empire was a hollow shell of its former self. The Byzantine state had less than a decade to run before being wrecked by the terrible blow of the Fourth Crusade.

Tancred's one capable ally, the pope, was eighty-seven, in frail health, and unlikely to be of any help in the coming storm. The Sicilian king struggled bravely on alone. In the summer of 1193 he crossed to the mainland and began to prepare his defenses, but most of the peninsula was in open revolt, and the few towns that weren't had an air of defeatism. Yet with a combination of diplomacy, bribes, and shows of military force, Tancred slowly began to make progress in restoring his authority.

Had he continued, there might have been a chance to stop Henry, but in the midst of his campaign he caught a fever. He returned to Palermo in the hopes that the climate would improve his health, but it only got worse. In early February his eighteen-year-old son and heir died. A few days later the grieving Tancred followed him to the grave.

Without him there was no hope for Sicily. The sudden death of both king and heir robbed the kingdom of its will to resist. Tancred's three-year-old son, William III, was crowned, but it was a depressing ceremony. Those attending were more intent on coming to terms with Henry than fighting him, and even Tancred's queen, Sibylla, recognized that the end had come. She installed herself and her son in a castle and waited for the final blow to fall.

It didn't take long. Henry's progress through Italy was more triumphal procession than military campaign. Most cities threw open their gates and willingly turned over hostages as a guarantee of good behavior. Naples, which had bravely resisted the last invasion, capitulated before the first German soldier arrived. Without the energy of Tancred, morale everywhere had collapsed. In October Henry crossed to Messina after offering the city generous tax breaks to soften it up, and landed in Sicily unopposed. A month later the abandoned Sibylla surrendered and Henry entered into Palermo. After only six decades, Hauteville rule in Sicily had come to an end.

Henry VI was crowned on Christmas Day 1194 with Queen Sibylla and young William III in attendance, probably watching with a mixture of relief and sadness. The German emperor had been surprisingly mild in his treatment of the deposed Normans, promising adequate estates for them to live out their lives in a comfortable style. There was a vague hope that a distant emperor would be a moderate ruler and his kindness to the queen supported that. Only four days after the coronation, however, Henry abruptly changed tactics. Claiming an assassination plot, which may or may not have been the case, he had Sibylla and young William III arrested and shipped off to Germany. Any Norman noble who had attended King Tancred's coronation was rounded up and executed, while the emperor's tax officials looted the island. The Norman treasury at Palermo was packed onto mules and sent north, where the most famous pieces (among them King Roger's coronation cloak) still remain.

For Queen Sibylla at least, there was a happy ending. After five years in captivity she was released to live out the rest of her life in obscurity. Her son, William III, however, wasn't so fortunate. The last Norman king of Sicily died in a German prison. Some sources say he was castrated and blinded on Henry's orders, others that he was forcibly tonsured. Perhaps it was both; either way he was dead within four years.

The Norman kingdom of Sicily was only sixty-four years old when it died, and for the people of Sicily the loss was tremendous. The island was, as its most perceptive citizens had feared, lost within the vast German Empire. Never again would it run its own affairs or have the luxury of native rule. Henceforth it would always be just a part of some larger kingdom or state. The real tragedy in this was that its own rulers had thrown away that independence.

The Achilles heel of Norman Sicily had always been the absolute power of its kings. Everything depended on the character of the person on the throne. Under the brilliant Rogers, Sicily was wealthy and prosperous; under the Williams it actively decayed. Tancred may have made a worthy king, but he didn't have the chance to prove himself. Norman Sicily had blazed brilliantly; the island would never be so prosperous or happy again.

Chapter Seventeen

STUPOR MUNDI AND THE
NORMAN SUNSET

There was one central figure of the Norman kingdom that was conspicuously absent during its demise. Constance, William II's aunt who was promised the kingdom by her nephew, and on whose behalf Henry VI had invaded and conquered Sicily, missed his coronation.

Although she was of Hauteville blood, and technically the ruler of Sicily, Constance did not cross over the straits for the festivities. She was on the mainland, where she gave birth to Henry's only son. Because he was baptized in Assisi, he was known locally as the 'son of Apulia', and embraced by the people of southern Italy. He was given the Christian names of Frederick and Roger in honor of his two grandfathers, and this in many ways symbolized the hopes for him: to unite the prowess and energy of Barbarossa with the administrative statesmanship of Roger II.

The expectations were dizzying. His birth was celebrated like that of a new Messiah. His reign was forecast to be like a sun without a cloud, never to suffer eclipse.

Frederick's youth was spent in gorgeous palaces, surrounded by his Muslim tutors and every luxury, but he never knew a sunny childhood. At the age of two his father died, and he was sent to Germany to claim its crown. On the way it was discovered that his uncle Philip of Swabia was disputing his elevation and had started a civil war. Frederick was returned to Palermo where he was crowned as king on May 17, 1198. His mother, Constance, ruled as regent and, given the unpopularity of the Germans, she tried to placate her subjects by dissolving all ties to the empire. The overbearing imperial counselors were sent home, and Frederick's claims to the imperial throne were renounced. Unfortunately, she herself died the same year, and the now orphaned three-and-a-half-year-old Frederick was shuttled off to be put in the care of the pope.

As a dependent of the papal court, his fancy titles seemed like a hollow mockery, but worse humiliations were in store. The elderly pope wasn't interested in restoring Frederick's German interests[1], and it soon became clear that he was powerless to protect Frederick's Italian territory as well. A German force sent by his uncle Philip managed to invade Naples, and with the help of Genoa, cross to Sicily and seize control of the government. The Germans didn't even bother to formally depose Frederick; they merely ignored him while pretending to reign in his name.

The captive king was completely neglected, left to roam the streets of Palermo, his daily food provided by wealthy citizens who alternated by week or month. For the young Frederick, the lessons of this childhood were clear. Success in life flowed not from titles or position, but from a willingness to seize what one wanted. Everyone around him tried to exploit him, so he trusted no one in return, keeping his cards close to the vest. Success, when it came, clearly belonged to those who were most selfish and brutal in pursuing their aims.

At the tender age of fourteen, Frederick's minority was declared over, and he officially took control of the Sicilian government. It was largely a title without power, and he addressed his court with a speech where both his frustration and his Messianic tendencies were on full display:

> "Assemble yourselves ye nations; muster hither and see if any sorrow be like mine. My parents died before I could know their caresses. I, the offspring of so august a union, was handed over to servants of all sorts, who presumed to draw lots for my garments and for my royal person... No king am I: I am ruled instead of ruling; I beg favors instead of granting them. Again and again I beseech you, O ye princes of the earth... set free the son of Caesar!"

While Frederick struggled to assert himself in Italy, a serious danger was brewing in Germany. His uncle Philip lost a long civil war to a noble named Otto of Brunswick, and the pope, who was supposed to be looking after Frederick's interests, crowned the rebel emperor. The thirty-four-year-old usurper in turn considered Frederick to be the paramount threat to his throne. The moment he was able, he invaded Italy to neutralize the danger. His armies swept through Calabria without opposition, while the sixteen-year-old Frederick scrambled for allies.

Surprisingly, the pope was first in line. Ever since the Normans had created a kingdom in southern Italy, the popes had used it as a bulwark against the German Empire. Since Frederick was heir to both crowns he represented the papal nightmare: Rome surrounded on the north and south by a single power. The pope had specifically crowned Otto to prevent that from happening, but now Otto had appeared in Italy, threatening to seize Sicily and make the nightmare a reality. In exchange for two promises – to go on crusade and to permanently separate the German and Sicilian thrones – the pope swung his support behind Frederick.

In the short run at least, the volte-face turned out brilliantly for the pope. Otto's invasion, which had seemed unstoppable, collapsed as quickly as it began, as the would-be conqueror found himself excommunicated and deposed in absentia. The triumphal campaign devolved into an undignified race with Frederick to see who could reach Germany first and claim the throne. The latter, meanwhile, dutifully turned the Sicilian government over to his wife, and then managed to beat Otto to the southwestern German city of Mainz.

Despite Frederick's greater claim, neither candidate really held the upper hand at first. The nobility of the south, who had never fully supported Otto, backed Frederick, but those of the north preferred the devil they knew to the Sicilian one they didn't. The two sides settled into a stalemate, not willing to risk going on the offensive until they were sure of some advantage. This caution was warranted. The first and only time their armies clashed, it was largely a draw until Otto's horse was wounded and his anxious attendants carried him off the field. A rumor spread that he had abandoned the army, and what started as a retreat turned into a rout. Otto withdrew to his family estates in the north, where he stubbornly held out for the next three years.

Frederick had himself re-crowned in the imperial capital of Aachen in the high summer of 1215. The celebration was marred somewhat by the fact that the pope was dragging his feet over offering the title of 'Emperor', but whether he was king or emperor, Frederick now faced the important question of where he would base himself. He controlled kingdoms at opposite ends of Europe separated by the Alps and a hostile band of Lombard states. Either Palermo or Aachen would become the epicenter of secular power in Western Europe.

If it were only a question of prestige, the choice would have been simple. The office of 'Emperor', successor of Char-

lemagne and – at least according to propaganda – the glory of
the ancient Roman Empire obviously outshone the kingdom
of Sicily. There were, however, other more practical consider-
ations. In Germany Frederick was a limited emperor, bound
by feudal responsibilities to nobles who had sided with him
not for loyalty's sake but to be rid of the former ruler. In Sicily, on the other hand, he was an absolute monarch, under
no laws but those he chose to make. He was also far more
at home in the south than he would ever be in the north.
His name may have been Teutonic, but Frederick II was a
product of the southern Normans. Palermo had raised him,
had formed his outlook and imagination. Now, when it came
time to choose a place to live, he returned home. During the
rest of his reign, some thirty-five more years, he would return
to Germany only once, and then only briefly.

The pope, predictably, was furious. One of the conditions
of papal support had been that Frederick would abandon
southern Italy to his son and confine himself to Germany,
so Frederick renewed his vow to go crusading in an attempt
to placate him. The gesture would have been more effective
if he had begun preparations at once, but the truth was that
Frederick had little interest in Jerusalem, and even less in
Christianity. He privately referred to Christians as 'swine' who
had polluted the Holy City, and reportedly said that the world
had been duped by three great impostors – Moses, Christ,
and Mohammed. At times he even stooped to mocking the
Christian components of his own army. On one campaign he
pointed to a field of wheat and said 'There grows your God' – a
derogatory reference to the communion wafer.

If he wasn't interested in religion, however, he was
inquisitive about nearly everything else. He had an insatiable
curiosity, and was willing, unlike most in his day, to criticize

authorities like Pliny, Hippocrates, and Aristotle if they disagreed with his observations. He collected animals of every kind, the more exotic the better, and assembled a menagerie complete with elephants, giraffes, camels, leopards, panthers, monkeys, bears, and a prized white cockatoo from the Sultan of Cairo. But he was no mere hobbyist. He approached everything scientifically, noting, for example, that the eye of a chicken-hawk enlarges when fixed on a target, and that the customary distinction between two kinds of falcon was incorrect. He compiled several treatises on hawking, classifying birds and studying their nesting, their migration patterns, and their daily habits.

Scholars from every nation were invited to his court. Experts in arithmetic, geometry, and algebra all wrote treatises dedicated to him. The medical sciences, nearly non-existent elsewhere in Europe, were subsidized from his personal treasury. A university was founded in Naples, one of only two places in Italy[2] where lectures on medicine were permitted. Prospective doctors had to be licensed by its board of experts before they could see any patients, allowing a uniform level of quality control. The university was endowed with a collection of Greek and Arabic texts so that (as Frederick himself put it) students might 'draw new water out of old wells'. Students were subsidized and protected on travels by imperial guards, all paid for at the king's expense, and they were attracted to Naples by cheap, subsidized loans.

Frederick was a prolific writer, composing several treatises on medicine, and even became a practicing physician himself. In between running affairs of state he found time to instruct veterinarians on the proper care of horses, attend the lectures of the most celebrated mathematician of the age, and conduct his own experiments by cutting open the abdominal cavities of cadavers to discover the function of the stomach and intestines.

He was also an accomplished poet fascinated by linguistics[3], and attempted to standardize Italian. Dante, who largely accomplished the task, gave Frederick much of the credit, and dubbed him the father of Italian poetry. He was fluent in all the languages of his kingdom: Italian, Greek, Latin, Arabic, German, and French.

Like his grandfather, Roger II, he was a great patron of the arts, filling the palaces (that he designed) with mosaics, marbles, paintings, and sculptures. His court in Palermo became the celebrated intellectual center of Europe, a Renaissance court two centuries before the Renaissance. No wonder his contemporaries referred to him as Stupor Mundi – the 'Wonder of the World'.

Although he ruled kingdoms at both ends of Europe, Frederick's attention was clearly focused on Sicily. The island had been devastated by civil wars and invasions, and large parts of it were depopulated. When he returned from Germany, he resettled it with veterans, and started building up industry on unused agricultural land. He then declared war on any traces of feudalism. Elders from every province of the kingdom were brought to the court and questioned about the traditional royal and common law of their homes. These were collated, edited to weed out contradictions, and used to make a constitution for the bureaucracy, defining the powers of the various officers of the state. Everything was minutely controlled, from the administration of brothels to the clothes certain of his subjects were allowed to wear. Justices were appointed that were dependent on the crown to lower the risk of corruption, and widows, orphans, and the poor were given free legal support. Although Frederick was an absolute ruler,[4] his constitution set the precedent of written law, and remained the basis of Sicilian law until the nineteenth century.

While Frederick reformed Sicily, events far outside his borders were beginning to force his attention to the Holy Land. Jerusalem had fallen in 1187, but both the Third and the disastrous Fourth Crusade had failed to recover it, so in 1217 a Fifth Crusade had been launched. Frederick had made vague promises to accompany it, but as usual had failed to do so. Despite the absence of a strong leader, however, the Crusaders managed to make some headway, causing the sultan to offer to surrender Jerusalem in exchange for a cessation of hostilities. The Crusaders, who expected Frederick to arrive imminently at the head of an army, refused the sultan's offer, but were then counterattacked and fled in disarray. Fair or not, everyone – both in the Holy Land and in Europe – blamed Frederick for the disaster.

The emperor didn't seem too put out, and continued to ignore his crusading vow in the face of mounting international pressure. In desperation the pope agreed to sweeten the pot. Yolanda, the thirteen-year-old heiress to the kingdom of Jerusalem, was unmarried, and Frederick was a widower. The two were wed in 1225, making him the official king of Jerusalem. Newly motivated, Frederick promised to launch his crusade before 1227 ended. He set the date for August, but caught a fever and postponed his departure until he recovered. The exasperated pope, who suspected that this was yet another delaying tactic, excommunicated him.

After a few months of negotiations failed to lift the interdict, Frederick decided to ignore the pope and at last set out on his long-delayed expedition. He made a strange crusader. An excommunicated skeptic who didn't even believe in the faith he was fighting for, with an army too small to accomplish much, he was ignored by the military orders of the Holy Land and had no hope of international support. But none of this bothered Frederick. Considering the small force available to him, diplomacy was the only option, and he was well aware of his own skills in that department.

When he landed in Acre, he impressed the messengers of the sultan with the breadth of his knowledge and his ability to speak with them in flawless Arabic. When the sultan sent learned men to him, they reported that he could easily converse with them on nearly every subject. A few weeks later, when the two monarchs met in person, the results were the same. The charmed sultan agreed to hand over Jerusalem (with the notable exception of the Dome of the Rock) along with a small coastal strip of territory. The next month Frederick entered into his newly-won city to take possession of it. He strode into the Holy Sepulchre alone, took the golden crown from the high altar and crowned himself king of Jerusalem.

Despite the surprising victory – no other crusade except the first had been successful – most of Europe viewed the entire matter with disgust. The city may have been temporarily in Christian hands (or Frederick's at least) but some of the holiest sites were still in Muslim hands. In addition, the city was virtually defenceless. It was surrounded by Muslim territory and, as part of the agreement, the Christians were prevented from building any walls. Anyone could see it was only a matter of time until it fell again.

All this was in addition to the fact that a heretic had recovered it. The day after Frederick's coronation the Bishop of Caesarea arrived and placed the city under interdict. The population was split between imperial supporters and those loyal to the pope, with most of the barons siding against Frederick. In the present situation the city was ungovernable, and Frederick left, never to return. Without him the city limped along another fifteen years before falling, as expected, to a Muslim attack.

Frederick had another good reason to hurry home. Reports had reached him in the Holy Land that his regent had started a war with the pope, and that a massive papal army had crossed into his territory. When he arrived in Italy, the monarch known for his justice, generosity, and diplomacy showed that he could also be quite ruthless. The papal armies were driven out and any who had cooperated with them were hunted down. Rebel barons were invited to talks and then seized. Dissidents were encased in lead and thrown into a furnace, while their wives were bricked up inside an Apulian fortress to die a lingering death.

The war between emperor and pope was deeply disturbing to the medieval mind, although opinion was divided on whom to blame. The Bishop of Lincoln called the pope the Antichrist while others cursed Frederick and schemed to assassinate him. Both sides had a sense that something was terribly wrong. The two heads of Christendom, spiritual and secular, should be allies, not enemies. When the two finally patched up a peace in 1230, most of Europe breathed a sigh of relief.

Peace, however, was only temporary. Frederick's son, Henry, rebelled against him, and tried to block the Alpine passes to Germany, but Frederick somehow managed to slip through and force the capitulation and imprisonment of his heir. Germany submitted to Frederick, but the Lombard cities of northern Italy, long a thorn in the imperial side, took the opportunity to rebel. The pope couldn't resist supporting them, and the old quarrel with the emperor sputtered back to life.

It took Frederick five long years of ruthless campaigning to break the Italian cities, and he celebrated by prematurely throwing himself an ancient Roman Triumph, complete with an elephant and public parade. The pope, deserted but not defeated, excommunicated him for the third time in

1239, and the encouraged Italian cities immediately rose up again. Frederick marched towards Rome, but wasn't willing to besiege the city and contented himself with sacking a few of the Papal States. Before he could threaten Rome, he discovered that the pope had died. Since his struggle was against an individual pontiff and not the Church he withdrew, hoping that the new pope would be better disposed and lift the excommunication.

Unfortunately for Frederick, the new pope, Innocent IV, was even more inflexible than his predecessor. Frederick managed to drive him out of Rome, but Innocent fled to Genoa and from his relative safety declared Frederick deposed. The emperor sent an army north, but at Parma it was routed. In the old days such a setback would hardly have mattered, but the fifty-four-year-old emperor was beginning to feel the strain of constant campaigning. A short time later his second son was captured and another son killed, and the double disaster broke something in the emperor. He became strangely indecisive, one moment talking of storming the pope's stronghold and the next of meekly submitting. Finally, in 1250 he renounced the world and took the simple cloak of a Cistercian monk. That winter on a trip through Apulia he became sick with dysentery. His decline was mercifully quick. He died on December 13, 1250. The body was taken to Palermo where it was laid to rest in a red porphyry sarcophagus beside his grandfather, Roger II.

Frederick was a polarizing figure in life, and in death he was no different. When Innocent IV heard that he was dead he said, "Let the heavens rejoice, and let the earth be glad; for the thunder and the tempest with which a powerful God has so long threatened your heads are changed by the death of that man into refreshing breezes and fertilizing dews". Dante agreed on account of the emperor's endless wars, and put him in the infernal city of Dis – the lowest circle of hell – confined with other heretics in a burning sepulcher. Everywhere he went he seemed to shock the sensibilities of those around him. His harem was the scandal of Christianity, and he was thoroughly eastern in his outlook and love of luxury.

But to others he was truly the wonder of the world, the most erudite, able and fascinating figure of his age. Even during his life, legends swirled around him. He would be the great emperor to announce the Day of Judgement, he would restore the Holy Sepulchre, burst the chains of Rome and establish a free nation. When he died in the midst of that struggle the common people refused to believe he was gone. In Germany they claimed that he was only sleeping beneath the Kyffhäuser Mountain and would return when ravens gather, to restore his empire to its former glory.

In truth, however, Frederick II makes for a poor German national hero. He was always more at home in Palermo than in Mainz or Aachen, and he abandoned Germany purely for more personal power. In a way he was the last flowering of the Norman kingdom of Sicily, warts and all – cosmopolitan, independent, and ultimately overlooked. During his lifetime, in 1215, King John of England signed the Magna Carta, a rightfully immortalized giant step towards modern democracy. Frederick's own contribution, the concept of a written constitution that would become the bedrock of all democratic reforms five hundred years after his death, has been largely forgotten.

If Frederick's reign was the Indian summer of Sicilian greatness, winter came quickly. Sixteen years after his death, Charles of Anjou invaded the island, killing both Frederick's son and grandson, bringing the Hohenstaufen[5] line – and that of Roger II – to an end. The kingdom remained territorially intact until the nineteenth century, tossed between the crowned heads of Europe. But it never again had a native monarch, or was anything more than a secondary concern of those who controlled it.

Epilogue

THE NORMAN LEGACY

By 1154, the Normans were disappearing. That year saw the death of Roger II, and although Norman rule would technically continue through Frederick II's reign, it was the beginning of the long decline of Hauteville rule in Sicily. In that year the Norman line in England had also been supplanted. Stephen of Blois, the Conqueror's grandson and the last full Norman king, had expired in 1154 and was succeeded by the first of the Angevin dynasty. Only in Bohemond's principality of Antioch did a direct Norman descendant of the founder still rule, but that state was a poor shadow of its former self.

Norman Antioch was surrounded by hostile powers, and only managed to survive thanks to the disunity of its enemies. Bohemond's descendants clung to power until 1268 when the invading Mongols brutally sacked the city, bringing the longest lasting crusader state to an end. The title, Prince of Antioch, continued to be claimed by Bohemond's family in exile, but it was of decreasing value and usually granted to junior members of the family. Eventually the title was acquired by a Portuguese prince in 1456, and when he was poisoned by his own mother-in-law the next year, no one bothered to claim it.

By then Norman rule was an anachronism, and the world itself was a vastly different place than that encountered by Rollo or William the Conqueror, or Robert Guiscard. Although they had not set out to do so, each of them had played a pivotal role in creating a new Europe.

The Norman achievement is all the more astonishing considering how brief it was. The Normans held sway only for the two centuries between the tenth and the twelfth. Norman rule in Sicily bloomed for barely two generations, and then lingered for another four decades without the same vitality. In the East, the Norman decline was considerably quicker. Despite clinging to life for almost two centuries, the principality of Antioch only had two effective rulers, the last of whom, Tancred, died prematurely in 1112.

Time diluted the restless energy of the Normans. They were always a minority in places that they ruled and were eventually absorbed by those they conquered. The Normans in England became English, and those in Sicily became Italian. Normandy itself was swallowed by France in 1204, and the native Normans disappeared into the surrounding population.

But for two magnificent generations, they had the world at their fingertips. William the Conqueror, Robert Guiscard, and the great count Roger were all contemporaries – as were their children William II of England, Bohemond of Antioch, and Roger II of Sicily. In each case an exceptional conqueror had been followed by an effective administrator who consolidated the gains and laid the foundations of a lasting state. In 1054 the three men who would become the most famous Normans were an illegitimate duke, a glorified pirate, and a penniless knight. A hundred years later their descendants ruled over the two most powerful and glittering courts of Europe, and the greatest of the Crusader states.

There was also a more enduring and important change. The Norman centuries of dominance had seen a fundamental shift.

No observer in the tenth century would have guessed that anything lasting would come out of Western Europe. It was surrounded by powerful Byzantine and Muslim neighbors, and fragmented into dozens of minor, decentralized states that incessantly squabbled and seemed incapable of unifying themselves. It was defensive and inward-looking, buffeted by Viking attacks from the north, Arab raids from the west, and Magyar invasions from the east. By the twelfth century that had changed. Europe was confident and expansive on all sides, beginning to roll back the Muslim conquest in both Spain[1] and Asia Minor. In the place of weak feudal states were centralized kingdoms poised for the explosive growth which would eventually see it dominate the globe.

The Normans are at the great tipping point of European history. It was their energy and daring that transformed Europe, their dynamism that was at the forefront of the new spirit of the Age. It's not a coincidence that the First Crusade was led by Norman princes and fought by Norman knights. Nor that successive reforming popes were propped up by Norman arms, or that armies as far apart as Asia Minor and Spain had Norman mercenaries at their core.

They are the great rags-to-riches story of the Middle Ages, a stark reminder of Virgil's maxim that fortune favors the bold. Between Hannibal and Napoleon there were few greater adventurers.

They demonstrate, if proof is needed, that exceptional individuals can change the course of history.

LIST OF EMPERORS

Carolingian Dynasty

800- 14	Charlemagne (Charles I)
814- 40	Louis I the Pious
840- 55	Lothair I
855- 75	Louis II
875- 77	Charles II (the Bald)
881- 7	Charles III (the Fat)

Guideschi Dynasty

891- 4	Guy III
894- 8	Lambert II

Non-Dynastic

896- 9	Arnulf
901- 5	Louis III
915- 24	Berengar

Saxon Dynasty

962- 73	Otto I the Great
973- 83	Otto II
996-1002	Otto III
1014- 24	Henry II

Salian Dynasty

1027- 39	Conrad II
1046- 56	Henry III
1084- 1105	Henry IV
1111- 25	Henry V

Non-Dynastic
  1133- 7   Lothair III

Hohenstaufen Dynasty (*non-dynastic)
  1155- 90   Frederick I Barbarossa
  1191- 7   Henry VI
  1209- 15   Otto IV*
  1220- 50   Frederick II

BYZANTINE EMPERORS

Macedonian Dynasty (867-1056)
  867-886   Basil I the Macedonian
  886-912   Leo VI the Wise
  912-913   Alexander
  913-959   VII the Purple-born
  920-959   Romanus I Lecapenus
  959-963   Romanus II
  963-969   Nicephorus II Phocas
  969-976   John I Tzimisces
  963-1025   Basil II the Bulgar-Slayer
  1025-1028   Constantine VIII
  1028-1034   Romanus III
  1034-1041   Michael IV
  1041-1042   Michael V
  1042   Zoë and Theodora
  1042-1055   Constantine IX
  1055-1056   Theodora

Non-Dynastic (1056-1059)

1056-1057	Michael VI the Old
1057-1059	Isaac I Comnenus

Ducas Dynasty (1059-1081)

1059-1067	Constantine X
1068-1071	Romanus IV Diogenes
1071-1078	Michael VII
1078-1081	Nicephorus III

Comneni Dynasty (1081-1185)

1081-1118	Alexius I Comnenus
1118-1143	John II the Beautiful
1143-1180	Manuel I
1180-1183	Alexius II
1183-1185	Andronicus I the Terrible

Angelus Dynasty (1185-1204)

1185-1195	Isaac II Angelus
1195-1203	Alexius III
1203-1204	Isaac II and Alexius IV

Non-Dynastic

1204 Alexius V the Bushy-eyebrowed

Crusader (Latin) Emperors till 1261

LIST OF POPES 10TH — 13TH C
with *antipopes** in italics

1024-1032	John XIX
1032-1044	Benedict IX
1045-1046	Gregory VI
1046-1047	Clement II
1047-1048	Benedict IX (restored)
1048	Damasus II
1049-1054	Leo IX
1055-1057	Victor II
1057-1058	Stephen IX (X)
1058-1059	*Benedict X*
1059-1061	Nicholas II
1061-1073	Alexander II
1061-1072	*Honorius II*
1073-1085	Gregory VII
1080-1100	*Clement III*
1086-1087	Victor III
1088-1099	Urban II
1099-1118	Paschal II
1100-1102	*Theodoric*
1102	*Albert*
1105	*Sylvester IV*
1118-1119	Gelasius II
1118-1121	*Gregory VIII*
1119-1124	Calixtus II
1124-1130	Honorius II
1124	*Celestine II*
1130-1143	Innocent II
1130-1138	Anacletus II
1138	*Victor IV*

1143-1144	Celestine II
1144-1145	Lucius II
1145-1153	Eugene III
1153-1154	Anastasius IV
1154-1159	Adrian IV
1159-1181	Alexander III
1159-1164	*Victor IV*
1164-1168	*Paschal III*
1168-1178	*Calixtus III*
1179-1180	*Innocent III*
1181-1185	Lucius III
1185-1187	Urban III
1187	Gregory VIII
1187-1191	Clement III
1191-1198	Celestine III
1198-1216	Innocent III
1216-1227	Honorius III
1227-1241	Gregory IX
1241	Celestine IV
1243-1254	Innocent IV
1254-1261	Alexander IV

*Occasionally two or more men claimed to be pope. Those not recognized as legitimate are called *antipopes*

BIBLIOGRAPHY

Primary Sources

Alighieri, Dante. *The Divine Comedy*. Trans. John Ciardi. New York: New American Library, 2003.

Choniates, Nicetas. *O City of Byzantium: Annals of Niketas Choniates*. Trans. Harry J. Magoulias. Detroit: Wayne State University Press, 1984

Comnena, Anna. *The Alexiad*. Trans. E. R. A. Sewter. New York: Penguin Books, 1969.

Falcandus, Hugo. *A History of the Tyrants of Sicily*. Trans. G. A. Loud and T. E. J. Wiedemann. Manchester: Manchester University Press, 1998.

Houts, Elisabeth van, ed. *The Normans in Europe*. Trans. Elisabeth van Houtes. New York: Manchester University Press, 2000.

Jumièges, William of. *The Gesta Normannorum Ducum of William of Jumièges, Orderic Vitalis, and Robert of Torigni: Volume 1: Introduction and Books I-IV*. Trans. Elisabeth M. C. van Houts. London: Oxford Medieval Texts, 1992.

Jumièges, William of. *The Gesta Normannorum Ducum of William of Jumièges, Orderic Vitalis, and Robert of Torigni: Volume 2: Books V-VIII*. Trans. Elisabeth M. C. van Houts. London: Oxford Medieval Texts, 1995.

Psellus, Michael. *Fourteen Byzantine Rulers*. Trans. E. R. A. Sewter. New York: Penguin Books, 1966.

Poitiers, William of. *The Gesta Guillelmi of William of Poitiers*. Trans. R. H. C. Davis and Marjorie Chibnall. London: Oxford Medieval Texts, 1998.

Savage, Anne, ed. *The Anglo-Saxon Chronicles*. Trans. Anne Savage. Wayne: BHB International Inc, 1997.

Vitalis, Ordericus. *The Ecclesiastical History of England and Normandy*. Trans. Thomas Forester. Charleston: BiblioBazaar, 2009

Modern Works

Barbera, Henry. *Medieval Sicily: The First Absolute State*. Brooklyn: Legas, 2000.

Barlow, Frank. *Edward the Confessor*. London: Yale University Press, 1997.

Benjamin, Sandra. *Sicily: Three Thousand Years of Human History*. Hanover: Steerforth Press, 2006.

Brown, Gordon S. *The Norman Conquest of Southern Italy and Sicily*. London: McFarland & Company, Inc., 2003.

Brown, R. Allen. *The Normans and the Norman Conquest*. Woodbridge: The Boydell Press, 1985.

Chibnall, Marjorie. *The Normans*. Malden: Blackwell Publishing, 2006.

Gibbon, Edward. *The Decline and Fall of the Roman Empire*. 7 vols. New York: Alfred A. Knopf, Inc., 1993.

Gravett, Christopher and David Nicolle. *The Normans: Warrior Knights and their Castles*. New York: Osprey Publishing Ltd., 2007.

Kreutz, Barbara M. *Before the Normans: Southern Italy in the Ninth & Tenth Centuries*. Philadelphia: University of Pennsylvania Press, 1991.

Neveux, François. *A Brief History of The Normans: The conquests that changed the face of Europe*. Trans. Howard Curtis. Philadelphia: Running Press, 2008.

Norwich, John Julius. *The Normans In Sicily: The magnificent story of 'the other Norman Conquest'*. New York: Penguin Books, 1970.

Runciman, Steven. *A History of the Crusades, Volume 1*. Cambridge: Cambridge University Press, 1951.

ENDNOTES

Chapter One

1. The modern term for the eastern half of the Roman Empire. It was also sometimes referred to simply as 'Byzantium'. See note *On Romans, Holy Romans, and Byzantines.*

2. Although originally a late classical term meaning 'Arab', by the Middle Ages the word Saracen had become a generic phrase for any (Muslim) subject of the Islamic caliph.

3. Vikings who were seized with an uncontrollable rage in the heat of battle were called 'berserkers'. They would occasionally bite through their shields, ignore even the most hideous wounds and kill friends and foe alike indiscriminately.

4. Muslim forces entered Spain in AD 711. By the end of the century they had largely conquered it, and would continue to hold parts of it until the *Reconquista* of Ferdinand and Isabella succeeded in evicting them in 1492.

5. The Northumbrian Ælla and the East Anglican Edmund. They were subjected to the 'blood eagle', a brutal form of torture where the ribs were broken near the spine and the lungs were pulled out through the wounds to resemble a blood-stained pair of wings. The still-living victim was then left to expire.

6. Historians usually refer to this new state as the 'Holy Roman Empire' to distinguish it from the earlier empire of the same name. See note *On Romans, Holy Romans, and Byzantines.*

Chapter Two

1. These numbers are provided by our lone eyewitness source, Abbo Cennus. Most modern historians view this as an exaggeration, however, putting the number somewhere between 10-15,000. In either case, it was the largest Viking invasion yet seen on the Continent.

2. Rollo's ancestry is a matter of some contention between Denmark and Norway. The earliest source refers to him as Danish, but calls all Vikings 'Danes', while the 12th-century Norse sagas claim that he was Norwegian. The Normans themselves were split on the matter. Since medieval sources generally gave him a Norwegian ancestry when they bothered to distinguish between different groups of Vikings, I've sided with Norway.

3. Vikings nearly always fought on foot. Horses were only used to carry arms, and occasionally men, over long distances. Viking ponies,

therefore, tended to be undersized by European standards.

4. Charlemagne's empire had crumbled to the point where no emperor was recognized. Charles had been crowned simply as 'king' of Western Francia, i.e. the French-speaking lands of the old empire.

5. After discovering that a free white garment was given to those who received the sacrament, some of Rollo's men were caught having themselves baptized numerous times.

Chapter Three

1. This is a clever Anglo-Saxon pun on the king's name. 'Ethelred' means 'wise counsel' and 'Unraed' translates to something like 'un-counseled'. One can imagine an exasperated English farmer thinking 'Wise Counsel? More like *Un*-Counseled'.

2. One of these was Olaf Haraldsson, the future king and patron saint of Norway.

3. The Fatimid Caliphate was a Shia state whose leaders claimed descent from Mohammed's daughter Fatima. Although based in Egypt, they had captured Jerusalem in AD 969.

4. Including a young William de Hauteville who was soon to earn the epithet 'Iron-arm'. See chapter 8.

Chapter Five

1. So many men were drowned that a mill several miles downstream was clogged with the bodies and had to cease operation.

2. and quite short at four foot two inches.

3. Charlemagne's title of 'Roman' emperor was claimed by the German king Otto I in 962. Although it is usually known as the Holy Roman Empire, for the sake of clarity I refer to this state as the 'German' empire.

Chapter Six

1. Norman sources argue that Edward always intended William to be his heir. Even given his Norman sympathies, this is hard to believe. In fact, during the course of his reign Edward dangled the promise of succession to a number of individuals. It was a shrewd, if dangerous, way to counterbalance the Godwin family's influence.

2. According to Norman propaganda, Godwin choked on a piece of bread while angrily denying the old charge of his involvement in Alfred's murder.

3. The Welsh Marches were the rugged – and notoriously difficult to control –border between medieval England and Wales.

4. He arrived to find that Malcom III had recently killed the High King Macbeth.

Chapter Seven

1. Basil II. The brilliant Macedonian Dynasty had ruled over the

Byzantine Empire for nearly two centuries.
2. Supposedly the Empress Zoë wanted to marry him, and when he refused, she threw him into a dungeon from which he (of course) had a daring escape.

Chapter Eight
1. The Hippodrome was the imperial capital's main stadium. It was originally designed for chariot races, but came to be used for nearly every important public ceremony. Defeated enemies, failed rebels, or overthrown emperors were often paraded there in humiliating fashion before being executed.

Chapter Nine
1. Sybaris was famous for its hedonism. We get the modern word 'sybaritic' meaning self-indulgent or overly luxurious from it.
2. Lands surrounding Rome and Ravenna ruled directly by the pope. See note on *The Papal States.*
3. See chapter 5.
4. Although the western half of the Roman Empire had collapsed in the fifth century, the eastern half (more commonly known as Byzantine) had re-conquered Italy in the sixth century. Guiscard's conquest of Bari ended nearly a thousand years of continued rule in Italy by the successors of Augustus Caesar.

Chapter Ten
1. On the coast of present day Albania.
2. Greek Fire, a flammable oil-based substance that could burn even while submerged, was considered a state secret. The presence of it onboard Venetian ships is an indication of how seriously the Byzantines considered the Norman threat.
3. More commonly known as the Castel Sant'Angelo, it had been fortified in the 5th century and served as the main papal stronghold.

Chapter Eleven
1. Modern Albania.
2. In present day Republic of Macedonia (also known as the Former Yugoslav Republic of Macedonia).
3. Borsa means purse – young Roger gained this nickname because he had the irritating habit of repeatedly counting his money.
4. The Hauteville family was well represented on the First Crusade. No less than six grandsons and two great-grandsons of old Tancred joined.
5. Depending on their importance (or lack of it), guests could be made to wait up to several weeks for an audience with the emperor.
6. The modern meaning of the term 'byzantine' – excessively complex and duplicitous – largely dates from this period. Most westerners believed the Byzantines had betrayed them, and blamed the 'treacherous

Greeks' for the disasters of subsequent crusades.

Chapter Twelve

1. The meeting took place on an old Roman bridge which is still called Ponte Guiscardo in Robert's honor.
2. The last military campaign he attempted was the 1091 invasion of Malta. When he captured its capital he tore off a portion of his checkered red-and-white banner and presented it to the Maltese. More than nine hundred years later it's still the base of the present-day Maltese flag.
3. She was a noblewoman from Piedmont whose main qualification as a perspective wife was that she was said to be fertile.

Chapter Thirteen

1. Feudal knights were only required to serve for a limited period of time each year. A strong lord could attempt to hold them longer, but even kings couldn't detain them indefinitely.
2. During his remarkable career, Bernard of Clairvaux was at the center of nearly every major event of the early twelfth century. He almost single-handedly launched the second Crusade, is remembered as an honorary founder of the Cistercian order, and was responsible for the founding of more than 150 monasteries throughout Europe.
3. Encouraged of course by Sicilian gold.
4. This is the depiction of Christ as an all-powerful judge, frequently portrayed in the domes of 10th -century Byzantine churches.
5. According to Edward Gibbon he appeared 'in war ignorant of peace, and in peace incapable of war'.
6. In present day Serbia which was then part of the medieval Kingdom of Hungary.
7. A Venetian-led Crusader army sacked Constantinople in 1204, destroying Christendom's greatest city.
8. Roger's conspicuous failure to go on crusade – as well as the harem of Muslim women he kept – earned him this nickname.

Chapter Fourteen

1. This was over a hundred years after the Great Schism which 'permanently' split the church into estranged Catholic and Orthodox halves.
2. The instillation of a Norman pope, however, would have serious future consequences as it offended the German emperor, Barbarossa. See chapter 15.

Chapter Fifteen

1. One of the most impressive Crusader castles ever built, *Krak des Chevaliers*, is located on the coast of present day Syria. It was the most important stronghold of the crusader county of Tripoli.

Chapter Sixteen

1. There were a number of relics that purported to contain items from the Crucifixion. In Constantinople, for example, one could see the spear used to pierce Christ's side, the Crown of Thorns, the True Cross, Christ's burial clothes, and even vials of his blood.
2. The legendary sword of King Arthur.

Chapter Seventeen

1. Papal policy was consistently the opposite – to keep Empire and Island as far apart as possible.
2. The other was Salerno.
3. According to legend, he ordered two nursemaids to raise their charges in silence to discover what humanity's natural language was. Regrettably both children are said to have died before the experiment could be completed.
4. His subjects called him 'the living law on earth'.
5. The name of Frederick's dynasty which ruled the German empire from 1138-1254.

Epilogue

1. The *Reconquista* was completed by Ferdinand and Isabella in 1492.

Also available from
Crux Publishing

The Sea Wolves:
A History of the Vikings

by Lars Brownworth

"An axe age, a wind age, a wolf age". Thus the Vikings described Ragnarok – the end of the world – a time of destruction and death that would follow three bitter years of ice and snow without the warmth of a summer. To Western Europeans during the two and a half terrifying centuries of Viking attacks, Ragnarok seemed at hand. The long winter began in the eighth century, when Norse warriors struck the English isle of Lindisfarne, and in the traumatized words of the scholar Alcuin "laid waste the house of our hope, and trampled on the bodies of saints in the temple of God."

Wave after wave of Norse 'sea-wolves' followed in search of plunder, land, or a glorious death in battle. Much of the British Isles fell before their swords, and the continental capitals of Paris and Aachen were sacked. Turning east, they swept down the uncharted rivers of central Europe, captured Kiev and clashed with mighty Constantinople, the capital of the Byzantine Empire.

But there is more to the Viking story than brute force. They were makers of law – the term itself comes from an Old Norse word – and they introduced a novel form of trial by jury to England. They were also sophisticated merchants and explorers who settled Iceland, founded Dublin, and established a trading network that stretched from Baghdad to the coast of North America.

In *The Sea Wolves*, Lars Brownworth brings to life this extraordinary Norse world of epic poets, heroes, and travelers through the stories of the great Viking figures. Among others, Leif the Lucky who discovered a new world, Ragnar Lodbrok the scourge of France, Eric Bloodaxe who ruled in York, and the crafty Harald Hardrada illuminate the saga of the Viking age – a time which "has passed away, and grown dark under the cover of night".

COMING IN AUTUMN 2014

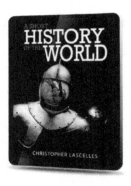

A Short History of the World

by Christopher Lascelles

'A clearly written, remarkably comprehensive guide to the greatest story on Earth – man's journey from the earliest times to the modern day. Highly recommended.'
DAN JONES, author of *The Plantagenets: The Kings Who Made England*

A Short History of the World is a short and easy-to-read history book that relates the history of our world from the Big Bang to the present day. It assumes no prior knowledge of past events and 32 maps have been especially drawn to give the reader a better understanding of where events occurred.

The book's purpose is not to come up with any ground-breaking new historical theories. Instead it aims to give a broad overview of the key events so that non-historians will feel less embarrassed about their lack of historical knowledge when discussing the past. The result is a history book that is reassuringly epic in scope but refreshingly short in length – an excellent place to start to bring your knowledge of world history up to scratch!

the thing about Islam

exposing the myths, facts and controversies

Islam in the twenty-first century is at the very heart of world affairs, including its conflicts. More than any other world religion it has sparked heated debate, its name associated with some of the greatest terrorist acts of our age.

Some argue it is an intolerant faith that condones violence. Others go further, maintaining that terrorist attacks in recent times have showed Islam to have an inherently evil core. At the same time Muslims across the world have been left feeling that they have been subjected to hostility and victimisation. They themselves insist that Islam is peaceful and compassionate.

With such diverging opinions and heated debate, it is sometimes hard to know whom and what to believe. the thing about Islam is an engaging and intelligently written introduction to the Islamic faith and people – a must-read for anybody looking for a simple introduction to the subject.

Made in the USA
Las Vegas, NV
19 May 2021